"There's no tragedy in life like the death of a child. Things never get back to the way they were."

- Dwight D. Eisenhower

After

LEARNING HOW TO LIVE
AFTER THE DEATH OF A CHILD

Ed Lee
With
Ronald K. Ottenad

After
Learning How to Live After the Death of a Child
Copyright © 2022 by Ed Lee and Ronald K. Ottenad

All rights reserved. This book or any portion thereof may not be reproduced or used in any manner whatsoever without the express written permission from Rooted Soul Ministries Inc., Long Beach, CA

ISBN: 978-0-9864325-4-5

Cover Image: Allen, Brett. *Big Blue,* Image used under license from Shutterstock.com

Printed in the United States of America

First Printing, 2022

To my wife, Michal,

your love and patience,

as I have learned to grieve

and integrate the loss of our son,

has made all the difference.

Thank you for walking with me

on this difficult journey.

Contents

1. An Unwanted Story   1
2. Before and After   7
3. The Aftermath   21
4. Searching for Answers   29
5. Duck Diving   39
6. Reaching Out   59
7. Learning To Surf   75
8. Riding On Rails   93
9. Forward Motion   107
10. Emilio's Life   123
    Dos And Don'ts   135
    Recommended Resources   141

CHAPTER ONE

An Unwanted Story

The story that follows is one I never wanted to tell, let alone live.

As parents, we never imagine having to endure the death of a child. The idea is unthinkable. We dedicate much of our energy to keeping our child safe. We do everything in our power to provide protection.

But not everything is in our power. Sometimes the unthinkable happens, and we are forced to live out a story we have done everything to avoid.

My son died in 2016. He took his own life. I have heard it said that when someone chooses to take their own life, they end up spreading onto everyone left behind the anguish that prompted the decision. Their effort to end the pain multiplies it. Having lived this story, I know this is true.

When my son first died, I did not want to talk about it. Verbalizing my thoughts and emotions only made the pain worse. I did not want to share my story with anyone. I would avoid telling people what had transpired if I could find a way to do so. I wasn't trying to pretend that my son's death did not happen

—I just did not know what to say when asked questions. What's more, I had no idea how to navigate all that I was thinking and feeling.

The experience felt like a bad dream, and I just wanted to wake up. Talking about it made it real.

I wanted desperately for it not to be real.

Unfortunately, none of us can live in a fantasy world, so we do the next best thing—avoid what we are really feeling. While all parents might be tempted to sink into this place after tragedy, men seem to be more prone to suppress our emotions and ignore painful reality. We often are brought up to push our feelings down and press on with life. When the feelings become too much to hide in the deep recesses of our hearts, we allow them to be expressed as anger, one of the acceptable feelings for men, or we find ways to numb them. As you will read, this was the route I initially chose.

That choice nearly destroyed me and brought me to a moment when I realized I needed help. I was blessed to have people to reach out to who were not afraid of my grief and who could assist me in discovering the way forward. Eventually, as I began to recognize the destructive way I was handling the death of my son, it dawned on me that I was living out a pattern many men fall into when their lives are interrupted by the unthinkable.

In order to break out of this pattern and form a new one, there were things I needed.

I needed to discover I was not alone, and that the

thoughts and feelings I had were quite normal and not a sign that I had gone over the edge.

I needed clarity that would help me resist the temptations that make the empty promise of relief only lead to more hurt and isolation. I needed to learn how to deal with my emotions rather than avoiding them.

I needed to surround myself with people who would guide me by pointing out the things that could offer real help and would eventually enable me to hope again. Hope was something I never imagined being able to feel again. I needed others who could envision a future I could not see.

I also needed the grace to allow me to go at my own pace. I needed encouragement to pursue a positive direction, but I also needed patience that would allow me to move when I was ready.

I eventually discovered all of these things, but not before I made a mess of my journey. I also needed a place where I would simply be honest about the mess that is left after the death of a child.

I did not need a perfect path to walk but encouragement to just keep walking.

As I read about grief, I realized it is often written from the perspective of a woman. What I really desired was to hear from a man who had walked through it and come out the other side. I did not want a psychologist telling me what the journey was like. I wanted to hear from another father who struggled just like I did, someone I could relate to, who I could feel understood by.

As I continued my journey, I began to meet other fathers living similar unthinkable stories, but who were a few years behind me on the path. I soon realized that when I shared my own story honestly and openly, these men were helped, knowing someone a few steps ahead could relate to their pain and offer a few hard-earned bits of guidance. I did not have all the answers. A lot of what I shared was simply telling them about the mistakes I had made and the help I had discovered. That was enough for me to shine some light on the path so they could walk forward.

Because I had not found the help I needed or the courage to ask for it until I was three years into my own grief journey, I decided I would find a way to tell it.

Right about that time, a friend of mine named Ron, who has played a significant part in my journey of grief, had written a book on male friendship called *The Risk Men: The Unexpected Rewards of Lifelong Friendship*. I got a copy as soon as it was published. I read it and enjoyed it.

As I finished the book, a thought occurred to me: maybe Ron could help me tell my story.

The next time we got together, I told him about how I wanted to help other parents, particularly fathers, keep from making the mistakes I have made by telling my story, and I wanted him to help me do it.

An Unwanted Story

Given my hesitancy to talk about what had happened, he was surprised I wanted to share my story in print—where anyone would be able to read it. I assured him I wanted to help others avoid some of the destructive choices I made, even if that meant feeling vulnerable and uncomfortable. It would help to redeem the bad choices I made early on.

It did not take much convincing for Ron to agree to help me. I am grateful for his willingness to not only help me write this book, but to accompany me as I have learned to integrate the death of my child into my life.

In these pages, I have sought to be as real and genuine as possible as I describe my son's death – the immediate devastation and the aftermath in the years that followed. Just because I have chosen to be vulnerable does not mean I have the freedom to tell the stories of others. I have refrained from using the names of the other family members in order to preserve their privacy and as a way to emphasize that this is my experience and perspective. I am not ascribing that everyone who was impacted by this tragedy felt like I did or dealt with it in the same way.

Grief affects everyone differently. This book shares the story of how it affected me and how I eventually learned to walk through it. While your grief, or the grief of someone you know, will not be exactly the same as mine, my hope is you will find in these pages the help and empathy you need to know you are not alone. I hope you discover those thoughts you have been afraid to speak out loud because you think they might be crazy are actually quite normal. I hope admitting my mistakes will help you avoid making the same ones and sharing the ways I found help will aid you in discovering your own. And I hope you feel the permission and patience to pursue healing at your own pace.

More than anything, if you or a friend are living an unthinkable story, I hope this book helps you believe there is a way forward.

CHAPTER TWO

Before and After

Every life-altering moment has a before and after. In the fall of 2016, I had no idea I'd experience a moment that would change my life forever. I just knew my "Before" was pretty good, and I had nothing to complain about.

I was born into a family of restaurateurs. As children, our parents taught my four brothers and me the ins and outs of running a restaurant. We learned how to work hard, cook tasty food, and take care of customers. These lessons were a gift, but the thing our parents most wanted to give us was access to opportunities unavailable in the country of their birth, China. They first moved to Brazil, where I was born and where we lived above the restaurant they owned. Eventually, they brought the family to the United States and opened a Chinese restaurant on Balboa Island in Orange County, California. We lived down the street and walked to work.

Our parents did the hard work of building a life in the States because they wanted to provide their sons with the ability to live the American Dream.

After

Thankfully, we would make the most of the opportunity they gave us. My oldest brother became a lawyer. The second in line is a doctor. The three younger brothers followed in our parents' footsteps and built a fast casual restaurant that reflected our heritage.

Our childhood was filled with the flavors of the places our family had come from, where we had lived, and where we had played. Growing up in and around Newport Beach, California, surfing became an important part of our lives. We spent many days catching waves at the 32nd Street Jetty and lots of weekends surfing in Baja California. There, we developed a love for fish tacos. They hit the spot after a morning of surfing off Rosarito Beach in Mexico.

All of these experiences gave birth to the restaurant two of my brothers and I started in 1988, Wahoo's Fish Taco. By the time the fall of 2016 rolled around, Wahoo's had grown from our original store in Costa Mesa, California, to over sixty stores in six states and two countries. Our parents built a life for us with their one restaurant. We took what they had given us and built a chain of restaurants.

In 1991, while working at our first store, a young woman came in and asked for help. Her tire was making a strange sound and she wanted me to make sure it was safe to drive. Our parents had ingrained in us to take care of our customers, so I was glad to assist. I felt doubly motivated since this woman happened to be quite cute. With flashlight in hand, I went out to examine her tire and found a rock lodged in the tread, which I quickly removed. Problem solved. The tire was attached to a Mercedes-Benz and the business card she handed me said she was a Doctor of Optometry. Both of these things were impressive, but what really caught my eye were her freckles. I would not forget her.

A year later, after our third store opened, this woman became a regular at this new location. She would bring her aunt dinner each Wednesday, and Wahoo's became part of the usual rotation of restaurants where she picked up food.

When I saw her face, and those cute freckles, I immediately remembered her and struck up a conversation. I learned that her name was Michal, and I was happy to discover she had remembered me as well. One thing led to another, and I asked her out for coffee. She said yes. When I went to pick her up on the morning of our date, rather than being ready to go, Michal invited me in and surprised me with a homemade breakfast. She must have known this was the way to a foodie's heart. And it worked, because that breakfast led to dating, and dating led to marriage. I felt lucky to have her become my wife. I have always said she must have been nuts to marry me.

As business grew, so did our family. We were blessed with two sons. From the moment my boys were born, I saw my primary identity as being their father. My passion for surfing, hanging out with my friends and cultivating new friendships took a back seat to being their dad. I wasn't thinking about pursuing my own interests. I was focused, like my parents, on creating a good life for my boys.

While I continued to give myself to operating and growing Wahoo's and developing other business opportunities, I did all I could to share life with my sons. I showed up and celebrated them when they had events at school. If they asked me to do something with them, I made sure I was there. I encouraged their pursuits, even when they were different from mine, and I made time and plans for us to create memories together—like eating at the best sushi places, going to sporting events, and enjoying family vacations. I was not a perfect father, but I did my best to parent my sons well.

In the fall of 2016, both of our boys were in the middle of the transition into manhood. It was a sweet time, and nothing gave me greater pleasure than being with them and sharing life. I was proud of the men they were becoming and excited to see how their lives would unfold. Neither of the boys showed any interest in the restaurant industry, which was fine by me. I wasn't looking to pass on the family business. What I wanted was for them to find a career that allowed them to use their gifts and experience satisfaction in their work. I was excited to see what they would discover in the next few years.

In this same season, I found new opportunities to share my knowledge and experience with people starting out in the restaurant industry. Wahoo's was not the only restaurant I had partnered to launch over the years. Where we lived, in Orange County, California, I had been gaining a reputation of being someone adept at starting up and establishing quality restaurants. The local newspaper even dubbed me Orange County's "Restaurant Whisperer." I liked this nickname. It fit me like a good wetsuit, because at that stage of life I found great satisfaction in helping younger restaurateurs give birth to their culinary dreams.

I had years of both success and failures that honed my knowledge of the business. I was happy to let others learn from my mistakes and glean from my success. I could help them achieve their dreams by anchoring them in the realities of the restaurant industry that I had been learning my entire life. This was just as satisfying as my own success, maybe even more so.

All of this—a successful business, a loving wife, the boys I loved and lived for, and the growing opportunity to mentor others—made up the "Before" of my life. I felt like I had it all. It was so good that the life-altering moment that would become the dividing line between the "Before" and "After" was simply unimaginable.

That moment came on December 5th, 2016. It was a Wednesday morning that began like most weekdays in our home. Soon after getting out of bed and putting on clothes, we pressed into the day. We greeted one another with the normal words, "Good Morning." We affirmed one another by saying, "I love you." We blessed one another with the wish to "Have a good day." After this ritual of kind and loving words, we headed in different directions: Michal to a doctor appointment, my son Emilio to school, me to work.

I cannot remember what happened during the first half of my workday. Compared to the events about to take place, whatever happened at work did not matter. All I remember was sitting down to have lunch at my desk, and I had just begun to eat when a call came through to me. It was a police officer. I have only received a call from a police officer two or three times in my life. The calls have never been good.

I braced myself. All the officer said was my son had been injured and was on his way to the hospital. He gave me the name of the hospital and asked me to meet them there.

He might have avoided giving me details or I might have been too alarmed to ask for them—I do not know. All I know is that I cleared the food off my desk and left for the hospital, thinking my son must have been in an accident on his way to school. I had no idea how badly he might be hurt. I told myself he was going to be okay, so I could keep calm.

The officer must have called me right away, because when I pulled onto the freeway I merged into traffic right behind a line of vehicles made up of an ambulance, a police car, and Michal's car. I knew immediately that the situation was not good.

Before and After

We were headed to the hospital together, but I still had no idea what had happened. Michal was in the car in front of me. I wanted to know what she knew, but I did not think of calling her cellphone. In shock, I focused on following the caravan to the hospital.

My heart raced. I tried to calm myself and keep my thoughts from wandering to all kinds of awful places. I kept telling myself to not get ahead of what I knew. We would be there soon enough. It would be okay.

When we got to the hospital, EMTs rushed Emilio into the emergency room. Before I could see him, Michal pulled me outside and told me our son was suffering from a gunshot wound. He had sought to take his own life. I could not believe what I was hearing. This possibility had never crossed my mind. I stood there thinking, *What? Impossible. Unbelievable.* It did not make any sense to me. My mind struggled to wrap itself around Michal's words.

My first instinct was to see my boy. I had entered a fog, probably thinking that seeing him would prove what I had been told was not true. I know my heart was hoping I would discover it was all a lie. But the hospital staff would not let us see him. They were evaluating Emilio and cleaning up his body. They were not ready to tell us anything because they were still trying to assess the situation. And they were not ready to let us see our child because they knew it was bad.

Our heads were spinning, without a complete picture of what had taken place. It felt disorienting

After

and unreal. In the absence of facts, questions rushed in. *How bad is it? What exactly happened? When will we know the truth?* We tried to come to terms with the fact that our son's life is in all likelihood ending.

With heads spinning and anxiety soaring, we were pulled aside by a police officer.

"We're beginning an investigation," one officer told us. "Take your time and try to be calm. But we'll need some things from your house, like your son's phone and computer."

They explained that certain items would help them determine what had taken place.

In fairness, the police officers sought to be as kind and compassionate as was possible in the moment. They had questions they were seeking to answer.

We had questions too! We would welcome any help in finding answers. In the moment, I did not comprehend all they were asking for. But I was hopeful they would help me put to rest the questions already swirling in my mind.

Soon after we were approached by the police officer, the doctor came out and approached us.

"You can see your son in a moment," he said. "But first, please come with me."

He showed us to a private room, where we sat down.

"I'm sorry to tell you that your son is gone," he explained. "He has no brainwaves."

Struggling to make sense of these words, the physician said that Emilio was physically alive, but mentally he was already dead. He was no longer cognitively present, but because he was young and strong, his body was functioning and fighting.

"Because of the strength of his physical body, we can keep him alive for a long time," we were told. "But we're going to have to make a choice about whether to continue to keep him on life support or whether we will let him go."

How do you comprehend such a thing, being given such a choice? We felt devastated and stunned. All I could do was take a deep breath. It was impossible to fathom that we were living out this moment. We needed to collect ourselves before we went to see Emilio.

Michal and I walked back outside, hoping our hearts and minds would catch up to what we had just been told. In the process, our thoughts turned to our other son. His life had been forever changed, and he did not even know it yet. We had to find a way to let him know. We wanted him to hear this from family.

I called one of my brothers and asked him to find our son and let him know what was taking place. It was a painful request for anyone to receive, but he agreed. We then called my mom and dad. We wanted them to know what was happening. It was hard getting the words out and telling them that their grandson had taken his own life. The same was true when we told my wife's mother, and other members of our family. As with us, it was hard for any of them to believe.

After

The family was now invited into this moment that would forever be a delineation of before and after. Letting family know did not chase away the isolation we were feeling, but we were no longer alone in this horrible, unimaginable moment.

We went back into the hospital to see our son. Entering that room was the hardest thing I have ever had to do. Our son was hooked up to life support and we could see the trauma to his body. The noise of the machines which were working to stabilize him and keep him alive created what felt like an unreal environment, one in which we never imagined finding our son.

We were being forced to come to terms with the fact that Emilio was brain dead, that our boy was already gone. We were also confronted with the choice to keep his body alive or let him go. Earlier in the day Emilio chose to take his life, and he succeeded in taking the part of him that made him who he was. Now we had to choose to take the part of him that remained. From what the doctor had explained to us, there was no other option but to let him go.

I hated the choice we were being asked to make.

The doctor also presented us with another painful choice. He informed us that our son did not have an organ donor sticker on his driver's license. But because he was 17 years old, we could choose to authorize donation. Because of how strong Emilio's body was, the physician assured us that his organs would be able to help many people.

I immediately began to weep.

Hearing the doctor speak about donating organs pierced my heart and caused my thoughts to stand still. In that moment, I did not have the capacity to choose anything. The doctor must have seen it on my face, because he then quickly offered, "You don't have to make the decision in this moment, but it will need to be made soon."

Being invited to donate my son's organs also brought images of the doctors cutting them out of his body. I could not bear the thought. It repulsed me. His body had already been wounded and broken. I could not stand to think of it being subjected to any more trauma.

The thought of it began to rile me up. Both the doctor and Michal tried to calm me down. I told the doctor I needed time to think about it, but I already knew in my gut I would not be able to do it. The thought of what he was asking made my stomach turn. My rational mind told me I should not be feeling this, that it would be a good thing for so many people. But in the moment, there was not much room for my rational mind.

My father's heart couldn't help but only consider my son. I could not bear to think of my boy's body suffering any more than it already had. I just couldn't. It is almost an impossible task to make such a decision in moments like this one, which is why we are encouraged to make them long before we find ourselves having to. My son had not indicated his choice. And we had no time to think about the one we were being given without the flood of emotions that were washing over us. Later, I would regret this decision, but in the moment, I could not do it.

At 4:00 p.m., just four hours after my lunch had been interrupted by a phone call from a police officer, we were asked to say goodbye to Emilio. Michal and I entered the room, still struggling to believe what was happening. We felt lost and confused. We felt frustrated and sad. All the emotions we could possibly imagine were wrapped up in a tangled ball. It was impossible to discern where one emotion began and another ended. We felt everything but were also unable to make sense of anything.

It was then that the doctor asked us if we had decided to let him go. We said yes, beginning the process of disconnecting him from life support. We reached out and touched his body one more time. We said our goodbyes and then the tears flowed.

When we left the room, the doctors and the police officers told us we needed to stay at the hospital until we were calm enough to drive home. The idea of sitting there, being unable to escape my overwhelming feelings, seemed impossible. I knew I had to get out of there. There were things to do, people to be called, and questions to answer. In my business life, I am a fixer. When a problem arises, I actively diagnose it and find a solution. I knew I would not be able to bring my son back, but I needed to get busy.

Before and After

Michal and I got in the car and began to drive home. On the way, a vehicle pulled up next to ours. The driver was a guy my older brother and partner knew. News had traveled fast. He had already heard about what happened. I looked over, and he made eye contact with me. Then pounded his chest with his fist as if to say, "I feel you, bro."

He tried to let us know he understood our pain and that we were not alone. But his compassion did not bring me comfort—it pissed me off. I thought, *You don't know me that well. How do you know what I feel?*

My heart desperately wanted to believe none of this was real, but the driver's gesture stripped me of any remaining ability to deny the truth. I had, in fact, received the phone call at lunch. I had followed Michal's car to the hospital, and she had told me that our son took his own life. The doctor told us that he was brain-dead, and then presented the hardest decision we have ever had to make. We touched Emilio one last time and then said goodbye. I wept.

Now this driver next to us, who I barely knew, confirmed that it all really happened. F-that! That's what my heart wanted to scream.

Behind the scream was the desire to believe this was all a horrible nightmare. I wanted desperately to wake up and find it had been nothing more than a terrible dream.

Instead, I was being forced to find a way to live in the *after*. As you will see, I have had both failures and successes.

After

CHAPTER THREE

The Aftermath

Sometimes, suicide is like a hurricane. It takes time for the energy to build up before it makes landfall. A person may have a history of depression, mental illness, suicidal thoughts, and even unsuccessful attempts. While this does not diminish the power and destruction of the storm, it does give the people who love them time to brace their hearts against the possibility they will take a direct hit.

Emilio's suicide was more like an earthquake. No warning. He did not suffer from depression or mental illness. He had no history of suicidal ideation, and he had never done anything harmful to himself. In an instant we found ourselves at the epicenter of a violent quake that sent shockwaves of destruction through the landscape of our lives. There was no time to brace our hearts.

Whether you have been hit by a hurricane or an earthquake, the energy released by either leaves piles of rubble in its wake. I wish I could say upon returning home I found a quiet place where I could give myself space to wrap my head around what had happened, or to let my heart catch up to all we had experienced.

Emilio took his life in his bedroom. A day before, our house was simply our home. Now, it was a space where a great trauma had taken place. It was also an investigation scene. I dared not go upstairs. Not because I was afraid of disturbing anything, but because doing so would make it more real. We did not turn on the lights. I did not want to see any part of the space.

Michal and I sat on the couch and wept. The dark silence was filled with deep sobs of sorrow. Our hearts were feeling the full impact of what our minds were struggling to believe. We were enveloped in the darkness of what had taken place just up the stairs, only a handful of hours before.

Occasionally, a neighbor who had heard what had happened would come to the house bearing food for our family. Their knock was like the ringing of a bell signaling the end of a round in boxing. It would signal me to lay down my sorrow, pull myself together, and answer the door.

I did not invite these people in. Instead, I stood in the doorway, listening as they offered their condolences. I found myself thanking them for words of comfort I did not want to hear. I did not want any of this.

I wanted my son.

I would then take the containers of food from their outstretched arms. I was not hungry. The thought of eating was the furthest thing from my mind. I am sure they knew this, but they also knew we would need to eat. They were seeking to meet a need we could not even acknowledge we had.

"Thank you," I would say. "We appreciate your kindness."

My words sounded hollow to me. I felt hollow. My heart was being ripped out. In this condition, it was hard to hold on to my neighbors' compassion. There was no place for it to sink in. I knew it would not always be like this, but right then, all I wanted to do was shut the door and return to the darkness. I wanted to sit next to Michal, sharing our disbelief and pain. I wanted to weep until there were no more tears. Maybe then, it would not hurt so bad.

What I really wanted was to wake up and find all this was not real.

Unfortunately, I was wide awake.

The space to simply sit in my sorrow did not last long. Very quickly, I found myself being forced to make decisions regarding cleaning up the aftermath of my son's decision to take his life. The police informed us that this was not something we could do ourselves, not that we would have wanted to. We would have to hire a hazmat team to do the work.

As the officers guided me in the next steps, they educated me on something I had never thought about and never wanted to know. The tasks they were asking of me were things I would not wish on my worst enemy. We not only had to give the police access to our son's private things, we had to hire a company to come and clean up the room where he had taken his life. We had to move out of our heart and into our head, because investing our emotions would have been too much. It would have crushed us. We simply moved forward, doing what we had to do.

How we would go about cleaning up his room was the first of many decisions we would have to make in the aftermath of the earthquake that rocked our world. We were forced to busy ourselves with what needed to be done. This reality kept us from being overwhelmed by what we were feeling. After someone has died, the first days and weeks are devoted to the tasks involved in letting others know what happened and planning a funeral to honor the life that was lost. The short-term busyness that results from all that needs to be done allows us to set aside sorrow so we can make needed decisions. For men, who often want to fix things and who are not always adept at experiencing their feelings, this can be a welcome distraction. It certainly was for me.

From the moment I left the hospital, even before I got home, I was drawn into all the decisions we had to make. While a few in our family already knew about what had happened, we had to figure out how we would tell the rest of our family and close friends. As the man on the freeway illustrated, if we did not find a way to tell them quickly, they would find out some other unintended way. I did not want them to find out like that. Because of their place in our lives, they deserved better.

This prompted me to think of others, rather than dwelling on my own feelings. It was needed in the very beginning. I think if I had been left to only hold my thoughts, I would have been swallowed up by the fog forming around my lack of understanding.

The simple but extremely difficult task of telling our friends and family caused me to realize that Michal and I were going to walk this journey in different ways. When it came to telling others, she was quite clear about what had happened. She told people Emilio had died by suicide. This made me angry. I could not bring myself to speak with such directness. This was not because I was embarrassed; it was because I could not understand it. I did not have any clarity, so I could not speak of it as if I did. I wanted to figure out the why of what had taken place before I talked about what had actually happened.

Maybe I was in denial. My head knew the facts. I had held my son's hand and said goodbye. I knew what Michal said was true, but my heart desperately wanted it not to be. By not speaking it out loud, I could allow part of me to continue to believe it wasn't true.

Because Michal and I had different approaches to sharing our news with others, I felt like we were not on the same page, at a time we desperately needed to be in sync. In addition to the conversations with family and friends, we had to decide what to post on social media. I chose to put a message on my Facebook page that gave no detail—it simply said thank you for your understanding as our family processes what we are going through. Those who knew of the situation would understand and those who didn't would hopefully respect our privacy. I avoided explaining because I simply did not know what to say, or maybe because I simply did not want to have to say it.

When news spread about our son's death, people surrounded us with love and care. For two months, friends and acquaintances brought us meals and called to give their condolences. I appreciated their desire to care for us. I also appreciated the distraction it offered. The conversations would begin with "I am so sorry" but soon would turn a bit awkward if we stayed with the subject of Emilio's death. Women would be too nurturing for me, often touching my arm and giving me a deep, compassionate look. I did not know what to do with this. For men, immediately after they gave their condolences, you could tell they did not know what to do next. They did not know how to fix it and they were uncomfortable with silence. So was I. In both cases, it was easier to turn the conversation to something else. I have no recollection of what we talked about. It did not matter. All I remember is being thankful we were talking about something other than my son's death.

Plans had to be made for the celebration of life. We knew it was necessary. We knew it was part of moving forward. But we also knew it is a milestone signifying the end of something—someone—incredibly important.

Planning the service distracted us from the pain. It kept us busy. It set our minds on planning and details. It focused us on the present moment and helped keep us from being overwhelmed by the shock. Planning the funeral presented a stark irony: it kept us from sinking too deeply and too quickly into our grief, and it forced us to confront the finality of our son's death.

During the funeral, I focused on the people who had come to remember and honor our son. While their presence was an affirmation that his life mattered and a comfort that they would care enough to be there, it also kept me from being fully present to my own grief. I worried about how it was all impacting them. I felt compelled to comfort those who came to comfort us. I had chosen to say a few words during the service, and I worried that I would not say the right things. I found myself worried about details: would there be enough food at the reception or how were his friends doing as they found themselves thrust into such a difficult circumstance? I felt responsible for how people would experience the day. Part of this might be cultural and part of this allowed me to not fully experience the day myself.

While we had people come alongside us and help with the details, looking back it probably would have been better to have delegated even more, so we could have been more present in the moment. But we wanted the service to honor Emilio well, and we wanted to be hospitable to the people who came to share our grief. They would have understood if we had been less hospitable and less organized, but I just could not do it. I needed to focus on others to get me through the day.

Interlaced in all of the activities were the questions I could not find answers to. I continued to struggle to make sense of what took place. Any quiet moment during the day, and nearly all night long, I would replay life with our son. I searched my mind for signs that he might choose to take his life. I relived interactions to see if I had missed anything. I reviewed my parenting to understand how I might have failed him. There had to be something I had not seen as life was unfolding that would explain what had happened. I could not keep my mind from searching for it.

Once the funeral was over, I no longer had the necessity of concentrating on the details or the need to be hospitable to keep me distracted from these thoughts. The only thing worse than having to plan your son's funeral was having the funeral over and being left in silence with your own thoughts. My hope was that news from the ongoing investigation by the police would break into the silence and help make sense of what had happened.

CHAPTER FOUR

Searching For Answers

As time went on, so did questions by law enforcement. They had immediately taken possession of Emilio's phone and computer, hoping to find answers. They began talking to teachers and school counselors, as well as his friends. They also interviewed Michal and me.

This scrutiny was welcomed. As I searched my mind night and day for answers, I came up empty. I wanted the police to provide a reason for what had happened. Maybe that would help me to make sense of it all and allow my mind to rest.

And I needed rest. I could not sleep because of the questions that filled my mind and my inability to lay them down. Because I could not sleep, I drank massive amounts of coffee to keep me going throughout the day. This not only fueled my days, but it also fueled my sleepless nights, which created more opportunity to dwell on unanswerable questions. It was a vicious cycle.

This cycle caused deep fatigue for an entire year. It was not the good kind of fatigue you feel after a productive day's work. It was a heavy, wearisome kind of fatigue. I trudged through each day and dreaded each sleepless night. I felt stretched beyond my limits.

During this time, I never considered taking my life. Knowing of our deep anguish, I understood how ending my own life would only spread the pain onto others. But I did think about what a relief it would be if one day I simply did not wake up. I would not have to awaken again to the reality of what had happened. Maybe then I would be able to lay down this heavy weight and find rest.

Since I continued to wake up each morning, I hoped the investigation would provide the answers necessary to break out of this cycle of tiredness. The reality was, in the short term, the investigation was just adding to it. While the officers involved did their best to be compassionate, they also needed to be professional. They were seeking facts so they could find answers, and this search sometimes left us feeling as if they were interrogating us and the people who surrounded Emilio. At times, this led us to feel like we were suspects.

We wondered if they would somehow determine that this was all our fault. I feared that this would be the conclusion. Not because I was worried about the police, but because I did not want to believe I had contributed to the tragedy by something I did or did not do. And yet, if that was what the investigation found, as hard as it might be to accept, it would help to make sense of what happened.

It felt like a two-edged sword. No matter what the police discovered, it was going to cut us deeply. If they explained how I had contributed to my son's death, it would give me answers, but it would also painfully pierce my heart. And if they did not make any determinations, it would be equally painful, leaving me to continue to wrestle with unanswered questions.

The investigation took months. When it finally ended, they called me to come and pick up Emilio's computer and cellphone. I went thinking that they were finally going to give me answers to questions I had been grappling with since the day of his death. I expected the meeting to be like the warming of the earth by the rising sun that burns off the fog, increasing my ability to see clearly.

When the investigators explained what they had discovered, it amounted to nothing. On Emilio's phone and computer, they found evidence of his looking forward in life. He had made plans for a trip with his friends over Christmas break. That was just a few weeks away from when he took his life. They found plans for college, where he wanted to go to school, what he wanted to study, and what his intentions were after education. He wanted to be a doctor, possibly serving in underserved countries. The investigation found no evidence of any thoughts or plans to end his life.

When investigators talked to his friends and

teachers, what they discovered was a well-liked, well-adjusted kid. Emilio was the kind of friend who reached out to those on the fringe and pulled them into the circle. His friends felt loved and supported by him and enjoyed being with him. He was not a victim of bullying—just the opposite, he was embraced by friends and teachers alike. The people interviewed could not give any clues to what might have been going on in his mind that would have caused him to take his own life.

His teachers did not see any evidence of stress or undue expectation in Emilio. Though we are an Asian family, of Chinese and Japanese descent, we do not fit the typical stereotype of having high expectations for our children to strive to succeed, be the first in their class, or achieve perfect grades. This comes in part from my own journey that is a conglomeration of several cultures—Chinese, Brazilian, and the surf culture of Newport Beach—which led me on a meandering journey to find my own life's calling. I found success, but not through academics. I followed my passion and played to my strengths. I have always expected my boys to take a similar route, so it did not surprise me that the police found that pressure to be perfect did not play a role in what took place.

But I did expect them to find *something*. The more the officer talked, the more apparent it became that they had not found anything that would shed light on the questions I had been asking. In the end, the officer explained that in 1 percent of suicide cases, there is simply no clue or explanation for why the person chose to take their life. They said our son was part of that 1 percent.

This was disappointing and frustrating. I wanted the investigators to find something that would quiet the questions filling my mind. Instead, I received no answers. I was left alone to figure them out by myself.

By the time the investigation ended, so did much of the reaching out by others. The meals had stopped. Everyone who had given us their condolences and temporarily paused their lives to be with us, even if it was just to attend the funeral, was now moving on with life. Even though our world felt like it had come to a screeching halt, the reality is that it did not stop. People moved forward, even if we were not ready to ourselves. The busyness of life drew them away.

I do not believe we were forgotten, but I do imagine it got harder for others to know what to say after time had passed. The time for condolences had come to a close. Now we were left alone with our questions and sadness, and let's face it, most people are not very good at sitting in the tension of either. Part of me was okay with them not knowing how to talk about these things. I did not know how to do this. If they had wanted to talk, I am not sure I would have even known what to say. The emotion I felt most predominately was anger. When someone did take the risk of talking about our loss, my anger would spill out and I would see on their face they did not know what to do with it. Neither did I.

I found it was easier to simply not talk about the situation, and I was glad when others avoided the subject too. But what I needed more than anything was to talk. I needed to find people and places where I could dialogue about my anger. I needed to speak out loud the questions I was asking in my head—not so they could be answered, but so I could come to terms with the reality that they might never be. I needed to be able to share my sadness so it would not be so heavy. Even though each person's experience of grief and loss is unique, I needed to discover that I was not alone. And I needed to do this with people who did not feel the need to fix it, but who could simply sit in it with me.

All the things I needed do not seem to come naturally for men. We want to solve and fix, and when we cannot fix, we seek to avoid. Not being able to fix it means we have failed. Therefore, I could not ask for what I needed.

All of this made me feel alone and isolated. I was even isolated from the one person I should have been able to relate with the most, my wife. As I mentioned earlier, our journeys took entirely different directions. Michal was processing our loss in a totally different way than I was. I chalk this up in part to personality style, but also to the different ways that men and women often process grief. While women usually are more likely to move through grief by becoming aware of and expressing their feelings, men often deal with their grief by getting busy. It is not that we do not feel; it is that our feelings are running in the background as we focus on doing other things.

While I was alone in my thoughts and feelings, Michal was freely talking to others about what she was thinking and feeling. I could not understand this, because in my mind we could not clearly talk with others about the situation until we had some answers. When we were apart, this was not a big problem. When she invited her friends into what she was feeling and I was not there, I did not have to confront the fact that we were in different places. But when it came up when we were together, it made it difficult for me to not become angry that we were not in the same place.

For example, my career involves many events where we meet new people. In the year following our son's death, when people I met asked about my family, I spoke only of my wife and our older son. I still did not know what to say about what had happened, so I avoided the subject. I also avoided it because I could see the awkwardness it would immediately bring to the conversation. Here we were at a restaurant industry event that was supposed to be filled with good food and laughter, and I would be introducing a subject that would elicit feelings of awkwardness or even pity. It made me feel uncomfortable and put the other person in a position of having to choose just the right words to say. I wanted to avoid all the discomfort, for them and for me, so I did not say anything.

Michal, on the other hand, in these situations would be upfront about what had happened. She would say something like, "We have two sons, one is at UC Irvine, and the other is in heaven." She had no problem acknowledging Emilio's death. She was okay with how that might impact the conversation. This was not wrong; it just wasn't where I was, and it made me feel like we were not in step with one another.

Her response made me angry because I felt like it appeared that I was lying. I was not, of course. There is no obligation to reveal our deepest hurts, especially ones we are still trying to make sense of, to people at a dinner party. But the fact that Michal had no problem doing this, especially to people I had successfully avoided the subject with, left me feeling exposed. And I hated that.

Later, I would come to find out that it is not unusual for spouses to experience grief quite differently. And this is one reason so many marriages—approximately 80 percent—end in divorce after the death of a child. The partners feel disconnected from one another at the very time they need connection to hold them together.

In the disconnection, I began to make up stories in my mind about what Michal was thinking and feeling. When I heard her freely tell others about our son's death, I told myself the story that she had gotten over it. When I heard her talk about the peace she had knowing Emilio was in heaven, I made up a story that she was okay with what happened. And when I heard her talking about trusting God's goodness, I knew our stories were not the same. How could anyone—how could I—trust the goodness of a God who would not prevent the death of a child? The more stories I made up and told myself, the angrier I became.

It made sense to me why I felt alone and isolated from my friends and acquaintances. How could they understand what I was experiencing? How could they enter the fog I found myself fumbling around in? How could they know the profound sadness and loss I felt? How could they understand the depth of my anger? What I did not expect was to feel this disconnected from Michal.

Looking back now, I realize I needed to seek help from people who had walked this journey before me, or who had been trained to walk with others through grief. I needed people who could help me find my bearings in the middle of the fog I felt like I was groping around in. I needed to do this before I would be able to articulate what I was thinking and feeling to Michal and friends. But in the middle of the fog at that time, I could not recognize what I truly needed.

Instead, I allowed myself to become even more isolated. I kept searching for answers in my head and sidestepped conversations about what I was thinking and feeling. I did not believe anyone could understand. It felt as if I was on a journey I had to walk alone. The truth was, there was no need to walk it by myself. I simply did not know I had the choice of inviting someone to walk with me. I did not know there were people who could.

I was left alone holding a jumble of emotions, dominated by my anger. I was angry with the people who tried to show me compassion. I was angry with people who tried to help. I was angry at the people who said insensitive things. I was angry with people who did not say anything. I was angry with my wife. I was angry with myself. And I was angry with God.

At the end of the year, I could not see any clearer than when the year had begun. I just felt more alone. Rather than accepting the unanswerable questions, sitting with my emotions, and inviting others to be with me, I distracted myself by staying busy. Since thinking about these things had not brought me to a place where I could find answers to my questions or lay them down, maybe filling life with busyness would push them away and enable me to move on.

In actuality, I was just punting the ball down the field. Eventually, I would be confronted once again by the invitation to acknowledge all that I was thinking and feeling. And I would be challenged by my need to invite others to walk with me as I journeyed through my grief and loss. But at the time I was not aware enough to know these things were necessary and possible. Instead, I gave the ball a swift kick. It went sailing through the air, into the fog and out of sight.

CHAPTER FIVE

Duck Diving

People say the first year after the death of a loved one is the hardest. It is indeed a hard year. It is the year you walk through all the "firsts." Some of these we knew were coming and braced ourselves for them. Those days included our son's birthday, his class's high school graduation day, and the holidays.

All of these special days and events only served as reminders that our family was not whole anymore. They forcefully confronted us with the fact that our son was gone. The first year is filled with such days—more than you would expect.

Given we did not have any experience of integrating a loss like this into our lives, I think we handled the firsts better than we were prepared for by life. Intuitively, we gave ourselves permission to make decisions about what we wanted to do. We did not give into the "shoulds." Those are the things we all feel we should do because of the expectations of others, how it will reflect on you and your family, or the fact that it is the "right" thing to do.

Despite growing up in an Asian family, which

culturally can have a boatload of "shoulds," I have never been highly motivated by them. My parents might even say I was skilled at working around them. In the face of all these firsts related to our son's loss, this attitude served me well. I did not feel like I had to do anything that anyone expected me to do. I had the freedom to hold all these firsts the way I felt I could.

That meant not celebrating Thanksgiving, Christmas, or Emilio's birthday the way we always had. Some traditions we suspended, with the intent of picking them back up in the future. Others we decided to tone down. And some of our family rituals came to an end. They could not hold the same meaning without Emilio there. We understood that they might eventually be replaced by new traditions, but we did not feel the need to decide that during the year of firsts.

We just needed to get through it.

The only day we celebrated as normally as possible was our older son's birthday. We didn't want him to feel like he had been forgotten in the middle of this loss. We did not want him to feel as if his life had ended with his brother's death. We did our best to celebrate his birthday as we always had. We did this not because we "should," but because we wanted to. It wasn't the same without Emilio, but we did our best to make it special.

What we did not fully anticipate during that first year were the moments that snuck up on us. There are a whole bunch of firsts we never anticipated that wiped us out. Like the first time I went running without Emilio. Running and working out were activities we shared. I may not have been thinking about it as I laced up my shoes, but in the middle of the run, while passing a particular spot, it unexpectedly hit me: *I will never run with my son again.* The thought turned the run into an unexpected first.

Many such moments popped up completely out of the blue. A song would come on the radio, and the tears would begin to flow. A thought crossed my mind, and I wanted to share it with Emilio. Before I could stop by his room or send a text, I realized he was not there. My emotions were triggered by suddenly noticing the empty chair at the dinner table, going to a place we often went together, the taste of food he loved, a familiar smell that brought back a memory, or a sound that reminded me of my son. These moments reminded me of the life we lived together. They also made me keenly aware of all the life we would no longer share.

In moments like these, the grief rolled up on me like a massive wave and tossed me about. Because I did not see them coming, they are harder to prepare for. They were discovered in unforeseen places and unanticipated circumstances. Unlike the holidays, there was no time to decide what we wanted to do with them. We just had to walk through them as they came.

All these firsts, both the expected and unexpected, did make the first year very hard—brutal, in fact. But as hard as it was, I think the second year is even worse.

During the first year, a deceased loved one is with you in a very particular way. Their death is a painful reality. They are no longer physically present, but their absence is a presence of sorts. It influences so much of how you are living. You are making all kinds of decisions about how to navigate life in their absence and how to walk through the firsts without them.

In the second year, much of this work has been completed. You have a year under your belt and have navigated through the newness of the loss. Now, there are fewer firsts. You are adjusting to a totally new rhythm. It is the rhythm of living life without them. Their absence is experienced at a whole new level.

In the days and weeks after Emilio's death, even though he was no longer physically present, he was with us in the people that surrounded us, the stories they told about him, and the memories we shared, especially leading up to and during his celebration of life. As I had said before, these things diminished greatly after the funeral as people got back to their normal lives, but they were still present, especially when a significant first was coming around. People knew it would be hard, and they would find meaningful ways to re-engage and let us know they were thinking about him and us. Eventually, as the year passed, these contacts and condolences slowed to a trickle.

In the second year, it felt like the water had been turned off. People understand the first year is hard and they do what they can to help you survive it. But most of us think that once you have gotten through the first year, it gets easier and support is not needed in the same way. I would have thought that before I lived it. In my experience, the second year was far harder. The need for support was just as great.

In the second year, we had to come to terms with the reality that we were going to live the rest of our lives without our son. This was something I never imagined having to do—children are not supposed to die before their parents. I did not choose this. And I did not want to have to integrate the death of my son into my life.

For me, the second year after Emilio's passing led me into deeper pain, and I did not handle it well. I didn't want to integrate the death of my son into my life. When I was somehow confronted with the need to do so, it felt like a "should" and when needed or wanted, I am good at finding a way around the "shoulds" of life.

Since I did not want to have to learn to live with his death, I got busy with my work. I had partnered with a very talented chef who had a vision of using his culinary skills to create restaurants that would also help people. It was a vision that would tap into my entrepreneurial temperament and all the skills I had gained in my years in the restaurant industry. It would require a great deal of time, energy, and attention. If it all came together, it would give birth to something that was more than just a great restaurant. It would be a business that would help people, especially children, by providing the tools and opportunities necessary to overcome the barriers brought on by homelessness. It could simultaneously turn a profit and turn lives around. This excited me and gave me a sense of purpose and direction.

The fact that it was not just another business, but a way of doing business that helped others, made it the perfect distraction from doing the work of grieving the death of my son. I told myself that this was such an important project and that I was doing a good thing by giving myself to it and ignoring what was going on inside of me.

Launching this particular establishment would take longer and be harder than any of the restaurants I had built before. It came with unexpected challenges and setbacks, which were both frustrations and problems that consumed my mind's capacity to think. This kept me from thinking about Emilio's death and my grief. Though not healthy, this was welcomed.

Every new challenge became a distraction, an excuse, an opportunity to give myself to this good work and keep me from having to embrace the harsh reality of how my son's death had forever changed my life. While I would not have said it or admitted it, I was operating with the idea that I could shove the painful emotions down deep enough that they would all go away.

When you are surfing and paddling out to the break, you have to navigate the waves that are coming onto shore. One of the ways to do this is to duck under them. Just before the waves break over you on your way out, you do what surfers call a duck dive, which is pushing your board beneath the surface and submerging yourself under the energy of the oncoming wave. You try to go deep enough that the energy of the water rolls over you. When it does, you pop back up to the surface in the calm that follows the wave. From there it is easy to start to paddle once again toward the break, where you can catch the next wave.

It takes years of practice to perfect your duck dive technique. I have gotten quite good at it.

Through my work, I was trying to duck under the wave of grief and let its energy roll over me. Unfortunately, while grief can come in waves, it is not surfing. You cannot submerge yourself deep enough to let it pass over you. To endure it, you have to swim through it. This was something I had yet to learn.

Besides work, the other place I looked to escape was in my passion for surfing. Since the time I moved to Newport Beach, surfing has been a part of my life. I love the thrill of riding the waves, but I also love how it feels to sit on your board and wait for them. It is a place of peace, where you can forget all that life holds on the land and simply focus on the waves that are forming. Looking for the next wave, you are able to simply be present to the moment, the movement, the anticipation of the ride to come.

During my hard season of loss, I would retreat to the ocean. It was a place I literally got to duck down beneath the waves and allow them to roll over me.

Even in this lifelong place of peace and escape, I would find myself bumping into the reality of our son's death. In these moments, I would be invited to integrate the loss into my life. Instead, I would find a way to resist.

I have a particular spot I have surfed for most of my life. It is familiar. I can look out on this stretch of coastline and know in an instant if the waves are good or not and if it is worth putting on the wetsuit and paddling out.

In having a spot like this, you get to know the surfers who frequent it. Between sets, you strike up conversations. In the years that followed Emilio's death, there was a younger man who often surfed my favorite spot. While waiting for the waves, he had a habit of asking about my family. I could not bring myself to tell him about the death of my son, so I would share as little as possible and turn the conversation back on him.

He was open about his life and family, which made me feel even worse that I was not. That did not keep me from deflecting and dodging his questions as best as I could. Part of me wanted to tell him about my family and our story, but I simply could not bring myself to speak the words.

Maybe I was afraid I would see the look on his face that I had seen on so many others. The look of pity or fear, because they were afraid that they would say the wrong thing. It could have been that I was afraid he would say the wrong thing and I would get angry. Maybe I was afraid telling him and the questions he might ask would lead to more unanswerable questions. Whatever was behind my inability to tell my story, I was always thankful when our conversations were interrupted by a set of waves that caught our attention or when one of us would catch one, separating us on the water and bringing our discussion to an end.

It bothered me that I was hiding the truth of my life from this man. It created a tension in me that even caused me to talk about it to someone who knew the whole story. He told me taking the risk of sharing what had happened to Emilio would be part of healing. He suggested that telling this guy, who I barely knew, might be a safe place to do it. I believed him. I even told him I knew I needed to do it. I just could not bring myself to do it.

Along with the busyness of work and trying my best to avoid telling my story, there were other ways I was trying to duck under the waves of grief and loss. I saw the loss and pain I felt as a problem, and I was set on fixing it. Some of the fixes I came up with put Michal and me at odds with one another.

To understand our differences, it is helpful to know a little about Michal's family. Her parents, being Americans of Japanese descent who lived in California, were caught up in the fear of World War II and sent to internment camps. Her father, who was 12 years old at the time, was sent to Jerome, Arkansas with his family of seven. They were loaded on a train that had its windows covered so they could not see where they were going and were given no indication of where they were being taken. When they arrived, they were housed in converted horse stalls, with tar paper walls and no heat. Coming from the temperate San Joaquin Valley, they were ill-prepared for the freezing conditions they encountered and within weeks of their arrival, his father contracted pneumonia and died. They would be later moved to the Rohwer Arkansas Relocation Center.

While Michal's father was subjected to harsh winters, her mother's family was sent to Poston, Arizona. Her mom was nine years old at the time. Here they were exposed to sweltering heat, often topping over 110 degrees and frequent sandstorms. Privacy was not to be found in the open showers and toilets. When it came to sustenance, often the only access they had to protein was horse meat.

Both families spent 3½ years in these relocation centers. This was a harsh injustice, one that could have led them to internalize anger and bitterness. But it did not. They made a decision, along with so many others, that they would not allow bitterness to seep into their heart. This was modeled to Michal's mom and dad by their parents, who knew resentment and hatred would only serve to mar the next generation.

Instead, they looked forward and chose to hope. They were not people who sought to duck beneath the waves. They chose to walk through their reality in a way that allowed them to be strengthened. The hardship was real, but rather than being crushed by it, they grew in their ability to withstand it. They understood that though this would always be a part of their story, it would not be their *whole* story.

This shaped the rest of their lives and gifted them with the ability to live a good and joy-filled life, free of bitterness, anger, or hate. This heritage of hopefulness also shaped their daughter's life. She was not seeking to submerge herself beneath the waves as she was navigating this dark chapter of her story; she was seeking to walk through it with hope.

This difference in how we approached the wave of grief that we were being buffeted by caused tensions between us, or at least within me.

It could be little things that revealed the vastly different way we were seeking to deal with the loss, like how we marked Emilio's birthday. Michal wanted to have a cake. For her, it was a way to honor him and spend time remembering the gift of his life. We had him with us for 17 years, and there are many good, life-giving memories. She was willing to press into the sadness of him not being here to celebrate his birthday, so that she could take hold of the reality that there is much goodness to remember and celebrate. She knew he was not physically present, but she also understood the cake created an opportunity to recognize in tangible ways that he is still with us in our memories and experiences.

I did not want a cake. I did not want to celebrate his birthday without him. It only reminded me that he was gone. I was still very angry about this fact. It would be easier to just not bring all this to the surface. The wave of grief was too powerful. It's not that I would not be thinking about my son on his birthday. I just had not come to the place where I could hold both the joy of his life and the pain of his death at the same time. Given my deep sadness, there was no reason for cake.

Neither of these approaches is wrong. I was learning in our differences that no two journeys of grief are the same. We were on the same path, sharing the same journey, but we were in very different places. I can see that more clearly now. Back then, I just felt frustrated that she did not see things as I saw them.

I was going to need to grow in my ability to honor our differences—in specific, honor Michal's unique journey through grief. There would be ample opportunities to do so.

One such opportunity was the house. I wanted to sell it, since this was the place where my son took his life. While I was not there when it happened, the image haunted me. The house reminded me of what had happened. Once, it had been a symbol of our life as a family. Now, it was a harsh reminder of the traumatic way my son had died. Selling the house, I hoped, would enable me to escape the pain this caused. It would allow me to duck down beneath the waves and escape what this space had now come to symbolize for me.

Michal viewed the house from a totally different perspective. Yes, it was the place of a horrible event, but it was also the home that held thousands of memories with our son. She did not want to let one day, one horrifying moment, rob us of these joyful recollections. She wanted to keep the house, because the memories that it held also held him.

When I realized we were not going to agree on selling the house, I began to talk about moving without selling. Maybe not forever, but long enough to let this wave pass. I began to float ideas of where we might move for a few years, or at least a season. Our oldest son could continue to live in our home. We did not have to sell it, but we could start somewhere fresh.

This was just another attempt to submerge myself and thankfully Michal resisted it. If there had been a good reason to go, she would have gone. But the balance of good reasons was in favor of staying put. Our oldest son was attending a nearby university. Our extended family was close by. Our work, life, and friends were all in that area. In a season of such significant loss, it would not be wise to let go of so many other things, even if it would seemingly ease the pain for a short season.

If we had sold the house or moved to a new city, I would have discovered that my pain went with me. A change of location cannot erase the loss. But at the time, I wanted to see if it could. I had no trouble convincing myself that indeed it would.

I did have trouble convincing Michal. She was not going to sell or move, and she had an ally in our older son, who also wanted to keep the house. I was outnumbered. Much to my disappointment at the time, we stayed in the house.

I was going to have to find another way to dip beneath this seemingly unbearable wave.

Business was doing an adequate job of keeping thoughts of my son's death at bay during the day. All the decisions that needed to be made and all the details that had to be taken care of to launch the new restaurant kept my mind swirling and my emotions suppressed. I got lost in the work, and I was happy to do so. There was no movement toward integration of the death of my son, just pushing it down into the deep, where I hoped it would disappear.

Of course, it didn't.

At night, when I would get home, when both my body and mind would become still, it all came rushing up. My mind would fill with the questions that were still unanswered. As draining as it was to be caught in the cycle of trying to find the answers, that was better than the images that would come to my mind of the last few moments of my son's life in our house. Even though I had not actually been there, images had formed in my mind that I could not erase. Though I did not want to think about them, they just appeared. If I tried to chase them away, they just became even more vivid.

While the days allowed me to escape, I seemed powerless to do so at night. The questions and images robbed me of any ability to have a sense of peace in the evening and made it difficult to sleep.

I began to drink.

I have enjoyed a good glass of wine for much of my life. But now I was using wine to quiet the questions and chase away the images so I could actually rest. I would get home, pour myself a glass of wine, sit down in my chair and allow the enjoyment of the elixir to chase away all that was disturbing me.

It was another way to duck under the wave. And it worked—for a while.

What began as a glass or two increased over time. I went from a couple of glasses to a bottle and eventually to two. I had quite a collection of good wine, over 500 bottles at one point. I convinced myself that I was finally enjoying what I had collected. There was no reason to hold on to so many bottles of good wine.

But I did feel like I needed the effects of wine. It allowed me to quiet my mind. It allowed me to sleep. It allowed me to not be inundated by questions or haunted by images.

I did not think I was an alcoholic. I did not wake up in the morning thinking I needed a drink. I did not need it throughout the day. I did not neglect my work. Just the opposite, I threw myself into it. The busyness of work was sufficient to keep me beneath the wave of my grief.

It was only at night when things got quiet that I turned to a good glass of wine (or eight) to help me escape. It was more than just relaxing or taking the edge off; it was a way to let go of what I struggled to release when I was still and quiet.

This might not have been abuse, but it certainly was misuse. And while it provided momentary relief, it was not healthy or helpful.

It is very common to turn to something to escape the pain. What people turn to might be different—drugs, alcohol, gambling, pornography, overeating—but the reason for turning to these is the same, to numb the pain. The hope is it will make it go away. What you discover is all it really does is push it off. The pain does not go away, it just gets compounded.

Day after day, my life looked the same. Get up and give myself to work, avoid talking about the death if at all possible, and let wine give me the ability to silence my mind and sleep.

These days built upon one another. They became weeks, months, and years. This rhythm did not just carry me through the second year since my son's death, but also ushered me through the third.

From the outside, it probably looked like I had been able to clean up the rubble from the earthquake that disrupted our family's life. Because my schedule was busy with work and events, and because I was not talking about my son's death or how it had impacted me, some might have even thought I had somehow gotten past it, returning to life as normal.

The truth is, you never get over it. There is no returning to normal. There is only the integration of the death and giving yourself to learning how to live in a new normal—both of which I had done my best to avoid.

I had not stood up and moved forward. I was stuck. I was sinking. I was drowning. I was just so good at hiding it, even from myself, that no one knew.

It all came to a head when I went in for my yearly physical in January of 2020. On the outside I looked healthy, fit even, but my checkup told a different story. All the alcohol I was drinking impacted my liver function, and the blood tests revealed the damage it was doing. The news was a wake-up call. Up till then, I had never really considered how all that wine might be impacting me. It was calming my thoughts at night, allowing my mind to rest, but now I was confronted with the brutal reality that this was coming at a cost. It was destroying my body.

Of course, the doctor asked me how much I had been drinking. It was hard to say, in part because I did not want to admit it, but also because when you are drinking that much you simply lose track. When I sat down with Michal to try and figure it out, we began talking about a recent event we had attended and asked the simple question: How much did I have that night?

The event took place 40 miles north of where we lived, in Los Angeles. It was my kind of event, centered around good food and good wine. It was the kind of event that was pouring fine wines that you do not want to pass up tasting. By this time, during all those nights of drinking a couple of bottles of wine, I had built up quite a tolerance. So, I did not think about the amount of wine I was consuming, I did not feel impaired, and I did not give a second thought to getting in the car to drive home when the event was over.

Michal and I started reflecting on how much wine I must have drunk that night. The glasses were not full pours, so we started adding up the ounces and converting them into glass equivalents. When we got through, it was apparent I had easily consumed ten glasses of wine, if not more.

This shocked me.

It is one thing to tell your doctor, "I probably drink a little too much." It is another thing to say, "One-night last week I drank 10 glasses." And then admit that night was not out of the ordinary. Drinking two bottles a night was the equivalent of 8 to 12 glasses. I was drinking way too much.

What hit me even harder was the realization that the night of the event, I had driven home. I had not been driving erratically, but I also knew it was not safe. I began to think about the danger I had put my wife in. I thought about the people who were in the cars next to me and the danger I had put them in. I could not bear the thought of causing an accident that might force someone else to go through what I had been dealing with the past three years. I knew I needed to stop.

Reflecting on that night, it became clear to me that the way I had been dealing with the death of my son could not continue. If I did not find another way to deal with my grief, it would only lead to more loss and possibly more death.

As painful as it was going to be, I knew I had to stop using alcohol to numb my pain. I had to figure out how to live with my son's death. I understood I had the power to choose to get off the path I had been walking.

I knew I could no longer submerge myself. I was going to have to walk through my grief. I felt like I was being forced to make a choice.

I had to choose to live.

After

CHAPTER SIX

Reaching Out

The time had come to face the truth. My drinking—which was my attempt to anesthetize my emotional pain—had spiraled out of control and was endangering my physical health. What's more, it was doing nothing to resolve my inner turmoil and anguish.

I knew something had to change. For three months, I tried to make the necessary adjustments to my life on my own. It soon became apparent that I would not be able to get very far by myself. I needed help.

I did not want to reach out to a counselor because I thought doing so would mean I was broken. Men do not want to be seen as broken, let alone admit it to themselves. I still believed I wasn't broken, so I convinced myself I didn't need a counselor.

Likewise, I did not want to attend a support group. The leader and members would want me to share about my son's death, which I didn't want to do—because I believed no one would understand what I was going through. This thought kept me isolated in my grief, which only added to the problem.

While my son's death had caused me to struggle with my faith (I had real problems with a God who would allow this to happen. How could God be loving and not intervene?), for some reason the thought of reaching out to a pastor felt safe. I had enough positive experiences with pastors to believe they would not judge me and would probably be able to help me. I thought they could help me find a solution without my having to admit I was broken or talk about my grief. This was naïve, but at least it allowed me to be willing to reach out for help.

I knew a handful of pastors from various seasons of my life. Some I grew up with, others I met in college, and a few I knew from churches I had attended. Not all of them were aware of what had happened to my son. I did not want to have to tell the whole story again, so I narrowed my list to only those who already knew the story. When I looked at who was left on my short list, I realized there was only one I felt really comfortable reaching out to. Our friendship was close enough that I felt fairly confident he would not judge me and might provide help.

This pastor's name was Ron. I had met him in the mid 80s while attending college in San Diego. We could not have been more different. I was from Newport Beach, and he was from California's San Joaquin Valley. I was a surfer and even after I tried to teach him, it was apparent he would never be. But we were both transfer students and that was enough for us to hit it off. Both of us only spent a short time at that school, going on to complete our educations elsewhere. Still, while there, we were good friends. When our time at the college was over, we quickly lost track of one another.

Our friendship had always meant something to me and even though we had not seen one another for years, I would look for Ron every time I passed through the San Joaquin Valley. Back in the day, you would have to call information or look through a phone book to find someone. Whenever I found myself going through the town where I thought he lived, I would search the White Pages for his name. When that did not produce results, I contacted the college to see if any records or contact information were available. Since he did not graduate from that school, they had lost track of him too. For over 25 years I had been looking for Ron with no luck.

Facebook finally provided the means of reconnection and in 2014—two years prior to my son's death—I reached out to the only Ron Ottenad I could find. Using Messenger, we shared short updates of where our lives had taken us. I was excited to find out he lived in Long Beach, just up the road from Newport Beach. Michal and I invited Ron and his wife over for dinner. I wanted my boys to meet my college friend I had told stories about and the man I had been searching for.

While we all sat around the dinner table, I told my sons a story from college that included Ron and how it had changed the way I perceived God's care for me.

It involved a surf competition Ron had talked me into signing up for. I had been hesitant because I was not sure how I would measure up, but Ron insisted I should do it. The competition would determine the roster for the college's surf team.

On the day of the meet, Ron showed up at my dorm room door ready to load my boards on his roof racks. I had stayed out late the night before and was not feeling well. The truth is, I was a bit hungover, but Ron was too naïve to know it.

"Ron, I'm not feeling so great," I told him. "I think I'm going to skip the event."

"C'mon, Ed, you're just nervous," Ron responded. "You're going to do this, and you're going to do great."

He was not going to let me chicken out and would not take no for an answer. While I protested, he continued to load my surfboards onto his car. Whether I felt like it or not, we were going and I was going to compete.

When my heat came around, there was no swell to speak of. If it had been any other day, and the ocean looked like this, I would not have even taken my boards off the car. This was a competition, however, so the competitors paddled out to where the break should be, even though there were no surfable waves.

As I sat there waiting, I found myself getting irritated. I didn't even want to come, and now I was sitting on my board on a flat ocean, waiting for nonexistent waves. The longer I sat there, the madder

I got at Ron for dragging me out of bed only to discover there was no surf. If he would have left me alone, I could have still been sleeping.

I looked to the shore, seething at Ron for making me do this, only to see him sitting there with his head down. This made me even angrier. I thought, *If he was going to drag me out here for this, the least he can do is watch. He's not even interested!*

About the time this was running through my head, I turned to see a perfect wave forming. I paddled into position and caught the wave. It was a great ride. When I finally bailed on the wave and turned back to the break, I could see other waves forming. I paddled back quickly and caught another. In the last seven minutes of the competition, I was able to catch three waves and score enough points to win the heat and move on to the next.

Victory did not do anything to diminish my frustration with Ron. By the time I made it back to where he sat on the beach, I was kicking sand.

"Ron, you dragged me out here and you weren't even paying attention when it was my turn," I said, with obvious irritation. "Do you even know that I won?"

Ron calmly responded, "Ed, I could see there were no waves. I was praying that God would send you some good waves to surf."

God had answered Ron's prayer and, in the process, I had discovered God cared about little things in our lives. He could meet us even in small, unimportant things like providing a good wave to surf. The experience changed the way I viewed God and what I was willing to pray about.

This was a story I had told my sons before, but it was meaningful to be able to tell it now with Ron sitting at the table. It was memories like this one that kept me looking for Ron all those years.

Once we were done eating, the boys excused themselves and left the four of us adults to catch up on life. At the end of the evening, just before Ron and his wife left, he reflected, "I don't know why it took you 25 years to track me down, since my last name is not very common. It seems like it should have been easier, but I wonder if God has brought us back together in this season for a purpose. I wonder if there is another beach he is going to have me sitting on where I will be invited to pray for you."

I could not help but wonder about the timing.

In the moment, both Ron and I thought there might be some other future potential victory where I would need the help of prayer to bring it about. Neither of us imagined I would lose my son less than two years later, or the struggle I would go through to come to terms with his death.

But that is where I found myself, so I called Ron and invited him to take his place on the beach.

The truth is, he had been connecting with me ever since he found out that Emilio had died. We had asked him to read a passage of Scripture at the funeral and he had been reaching out to me regularly over the past three years to meet up for coffee. We would get together every couple of months. He must have known I was struggling, but he never tried to force me to do anything. He would just make time to get together, and he let me go at my own pace. I guess that is what made him feel safe enough to call.

I felt embarrassed to call and tell him what I had been struggling with, but I knew I had to. When I told Ron how I had been dealing with my grief by working too much and drinking too much, there was no judgment. He did not offer me a quick fix. He did not share the five stages of grief or the three things you need to do to get over it. This was a bit frustrating at first. I wanted to fix the problem so I would not feel what I was feeling and therefore would not have to find ways to numb the pain. I wanted to deal with the issues that were presenting themselves and move on. Ron would end up inviting me to go deeper than that, deeper than I really wanted to go in the beginning. He patiently waited until I was ready.

Ron agreed to call me once a week to check in. I wanted accountability regarding my drinking. Ron was willing to be this for me, but just like at the surf competition, he was also going to offer me something I did not know I needed—a place where I could begin to talk about what I was thinking and feeling. He stressed up front that he was my friend, and eventually I might need other places to process Emilio's death. But he was willing to allow me to move into those places at my own speed, which was very slow. Talking to Ron once a week was a big enough step for me at that time.

In our conversations, Ron did not give me any answers; instead, he asked lots of questions. These were very helpful. I cannot remember the exact questions asked, or even the categories of the questions he asked. I wish I could because they were so valuable to me and I would like to share them with others. The questions he asked were not from some questionnaire or book; they were formed as he listened to me. They were not leading but they did often help me discover the next step. After I hung up the phone, I would often write one or two of them down so I could keep thinking about them. They helped me to think more clearly and deeply about what I was experiencing.

Sometimes, he was not even asking questions, but reflecting back to me what I was sharing. He was holding up a mirror that allowed me to see my own heart. It helped me recognize how I was thinking about what had happened, see how I was living, and be present with my own questions and frustrations.

Reflecting on what I had said, Ron often used different words to say the same thing, which helped me to see it from another angle or understand what I felt at a deeper level. I might say I was really angry, and he might reflect, "It sounds like you were really hurt." Hurt would be closer to the truth of what I was feeling. While it did not take away the hurt, it was helpful to identify the feeling and own it. Somehow, this made my emotions feel less heavy, even if it did not answer all my questions, remove all my frustrations, or chase away the pain.

Ron had no problem being present with me in my questions and frustrations. He did not get uncomfortable with unanswered questions, though he would acknowledge how hard it was to not have answers.

Even though he was a pastor, Ron did not seem bothered when I told him how mad I was at God or that I was not sure I wanted anything to do with him. Ron would just ask me if I had told God those things. I would have to admit I had not. God and I were not really talking and even if we were, I was not sure you could talk to God like that. Ron insisted not only that you could, but also that God welcomed it. He pointed to the Psalms of Lament to prove his point. He assured me God just wanted to be with me in the reality of my heart, which was hard for me to accept. I did not even want to be with myself in the reality of my heart. He told me to make my prayers about how angry I was with God and assured me I would not be struck by lightning. I did, and I wasn't. Doing this did not make me feel any less angry, but it did enable me to begin talking to God again.

Because Ron did not get freaked out by all that I brought to our conversations, I also became less freaked out. My questions, frustrations, and anger were still real, but they were losing their grip on me.

I still wanted to know why this tragedy happened and would often bring up my continued wrestling with the question. Ron asked me what would happen if I never found the answers. I hated the thought, but his asking the question began to open me to consider how I could move forward without answers. This was something I had not been willing to consider for the past three years.

Week to week, we often covered the same ground. There was no rushing through it. We would touch base on how my drinking was going, which was much more under control. I still enjoyed a glass of wine or two, but that was it—one or two, not ten. I felt good about this. At least one area of my life was changing for the better. I still struggled to be able to make sense of it all, but I was at least now talking about it. That was the biggest change, and I always felt better after we had talked.

While I still did not know where it would lead me, I began to feel like there was movement. When you have been stuck for so long, any movement, no matter how small, feels significant. In the movement I felt like I was regaining the ability to consider living.

Maybe the first decision anyone who loses a child has to make is this: Do you want to live or not? For the better part of three years, I would have been okay never waking up again. It would have been easier than dealing with the hurt. I would have never taken my life, but I also had a hard time imagining what living could look like after the death of my son. I knew I could not continue to just go through the motions of living, but I actually had to choose to live. In doing so, I would not be saying Emilio's death was okay, and I would not be leaving him behind. I would be learning to carry him forward with me as I chose to live into roles that were still important to me, like being a father, husband, son, brother, and friend. I definitely needed to choose to live for myself, but I also needed to choose to live for the rest of the people who I valued as part of my life.

I needed to live for my older son. Our lives, even as father and son, would be forever changed by the loss of his brother. But we could not stop living. The death of Emilio could not turn me into a disconnected, absent father, or keep us from growing our relationship with one another.

I also needed to live for my wife. We had built a life together, filled with many wonderful memories. I did not want the death of our son to cause the loss of that life as well. We had to learn how to live in the aftermath of this tragedy. We needed the freedom to continue to make new memories.

As I have already shared, the ways in which we were dealing with the death of our son were so different it had disconnected us. It was hard to talk to Michal about what I was thinking, feeling, and experiencing. I could not go directly to her and process my grief, and that made it difficult for us to move forward together. I needed a Ron in my life who was not as close to it all as she was, who would not be hurt or offended by what I said, who was not trying to make everything okay. In doing so, Ron nudged me to better understand myself and wrap my mind around my grief. This would eventually enable me to share these things with Michal, but I had to work to get to that place.

I think *nudged* is a good way to put it. Most men bristle if someone tries to tell them what they have to do or force them to take steps they are not ready to take. At least that is true for me. What I need is gentle nudging that allows me to become comfortable with an idea before I actually choose to make it, especially when it comes to asking for help or processing what I am feeling. I needed to be given the freedom to walk at my own pace.

In our weekly meetings, through his questions and reflections, Ron gave me little nudges in the right direction. I would eventually need to seek additional help. Ron knew it from the very beginning, but he also knew I was not ready. I needed the time and space to get comfortable enough to take the risk of admitting I was broken, seeking a counselor, and sharing my story with a group of people I did not know. The path to these places was in the process of being paved by the safety of our weekly conversations. I did not realize it at the time, but what my conversations with Ron were doing was tilling the soil of my heart and planting the seeds that would grow into the courage to take these next steps.

Before I would be ready to take them, I had to

come to some significant realizations. The first I had acted upon, before I knew how important it was. It is simply this: I could not do this alone. I had to have someone to walk with me. I believe this is true for everyone seeking to work through grief. The person who accompanies you on the recovery journey may not be the closest person to you. In fact, it is probably better if they are not.

If I were sitting down with someone who had experienced the loss of a child, the first question I would ask after listening to their story would be, "Who is your Ron?" Who is the person you feel safe enough with to talk to, who will not judge you, try to fix you, or be uncomfortable with what is really in your heart? I would then nudge them to reach out and talk to this supportive person on a regular basis, weekly if possible. You need a place where you can be heard and nudged. You need a Ron, someone who can sit on the beach and pray for you, even if prayer is the last thing you think you want.

I also had to accept the reality that I will be carrying this grief for the rest of my life. I spent several years trying to somehow get over it or past it. I expended a lot of energy and drank a lot of wine in an attempt to numb the pain. It took me all that time and energy to realize that what I was trying to do is not possible. The task at hand was not to be freed from the grief and pain, but to learn to live with it. I had to embrace that task.

Ron has shared an image with me that is helpful in

understanding what that task really looks like. It is a common image used to describe the real work of walking through loss. He said grief is like a ball and our lives are a container that holds it. In the beginning, when the loss is fresh, the ball of grief takes up a lot of the space in our container. It is a heavy, confusing jumble of emotions like sadness, anger, fear, anguish, and guilt. It is hard to have these kinds of emotions occupy so much of our internal space. What we instinctively try to do is shrink the ball of grief so that it is easier to hold, or we are able to discard it altogether.

What he said next was hard to hear. The ball never shrinks. Our grief never goes away. Instead of shrinking the ball, which is impossible, we can put our energy into growing our capacity to hold the grief. In a sense, we can make the container of our life larger, which does make the ball easier to carry. The ball takes up just as much space, but there is far more room in which it can be held. The ball's weight does not change, but it will feel lighter and easier to hold.

This concept reminds me of the Serenity Prayer, used often in recovery groups, which asks for the wisdom to know the difference between the things we can and cannot change. It asks for the serenity to accept the things we cannot change and the courage to change the things we can. I cannot change the reality of the death of my son, but I can choose to grow the container of my life to better hold the loss. In making this choice, I chose to live and move forward. It was a necessary and intentional choice.

My conversations with Ron were the beginning of the process of enlarging the container. But I could only give myself fully to this work when I accepted the fact I would not be getting over the death of my son.

This acceptance also led me to admit that I was indeed broken and in need of help. It was an unspoken reality when I first reached out to Ron. Both of us knew it, I just did not have to admit it up front, which made it easier to ask for his help. Eventually, months of weekly conversations gave me the courage to embrace my brokenness and need. I got to the point where I could admit it and speak it out loud. Rather than being my undoing, which was my fear, it felt like a relief to acknowledge this reality.

It helped that Ron kept assuring me we are all broken and in need of help. He was simply inviting me to accept my humanity. Embracing it enabled me to stop duck diving and take the necessary steps to deal with the waves of grief I had been experiencing since the death of my son. I had wanted the swells to cease, and the ocean to be in a state of perpetual calm. I now understood that this was not possible. These waves of grief would accompany me for the rest of my life. But I could learn to ride them out. I could grow the container of my life so they did not feel as powerful or destructive.

For some time, Ron had been making suggestions about where I might turn next. He was not pushy about it. He would just let me know there were places that might be of help when I was ready to take the next step.

I was now ready.

It was still hard to make the calls to these places, where I would eventually find a counselor and support groups, but it helped knowing Ron would be listening to what the experience had been like. And if I didn't like the support group or I was frustrated with what the counselor told me, I knew he would be more than willing to listen to me complain about it.

I would continue to need the weekly check-ins to keep moving forward.

CHAPTER SEVEN

Learning To Surf

While I love, respect and appreciate all of my brothers, I must confess, my oldest brother, Bismarck, has always been "The Man" to me. He was fourteen years my senior, but was more than an older brother. He was like a second father. He was the lawyer of the family, possessing a bright legal mind. We depended on him to make sound business decisions and to keep us out of trouble. He was fiercely loyal to his family, and always had my back. He frequently told me, "Ed, if you mess up, take ownership, fix it, and move forward." Those words have served me well in business and life.

If I got myself in a situation that I could not fix, I knew all I had to do was call Bismarck and he would step in and bail me out. He would fight on my behalf, and then chew me out afterward with the hope that the hard-earned wisdom would sink into my thick skull.

Over time, his hopes were fulfilled. The lessons were not wasted. I did grow in wisdom and learned to think about business and life like he did.

Unfortunately, Bismarck did not live to see this maturity in me. He died in an auto accident in May 1993, soon after we started Wahoo's, long before he could see what would become of it and me.

As the oldest brother, he helped hold the entire family together, and when the three of us set out to launch Wahoo's, he helped us get our start. He was one of our biggest supporters and cheerleaders. You can imagine the hole that was created when he died.

For me, I had lost a father figure. In an effort to make him proud, I tried to live out the wisdom he always sought to impart to me. I tried to step into his shoes. I took over some of the responsibilities he had filled in the family, and I looked out for his daughters. I also sought to always implement what he had ingrained in me: If you mess up, own it, fix it, and move forward.

In real and significant ways, I had messed up how I had handled my grief. I was willing to own it. I wanted to fix it and move forward.

You would have thought that losing a brother and father figure at a young age would have taught me to navigate grief. But the reality was, except for a short stint seeing a counselor when Bismarck died, which did not seem all that helpful, I had just stuffed it all down and put my energy into fixing what had to be fixed.

At the time of my brother's death we were getting Wahoo's off the ground, my youngest brother and I were about to be married, and there were some growing pains in learning all that is required to run a business. Normally, Bismarck would have been there to step in and make it right. He wasn't, so I did not feel the luxury of taking time to grieve. We had to run the business. I just pressed forward.

When Emilio died, the grief of his loss was piled on top of the unprocessed loss of my brother. Soon after my son died, a close friend of mine also died. There was loss upon loss. Experts who work with grieving individuals would call what I was experiencing "complicated grief," because of the different layers of loss and the kinds of loss represented. I was not thinking of it as complicated. I had come to the place of owning it. I knew I was broken. Now my plan was simple—get some help fixing it, so I could move forward.

The place Ron kept pointing me to was called Didi Hirsch Mental Health Services. With "mental health services" in the name of the organization, it is not hard to understand why it took me a while to open up to the idea of contacting them. Didi Hirsch provides therapy and support groups for people (and their families) who struggle with suicidal ideation. It had taken me a long time, with lots of gentle nudging from Ron, to reach out to this clinic.

The time between Ron's first mention of Didi Hirsch and when I finally reached out for help was not wasted, however. I did not know it at the time, but just like the conversations with Ron, other things made their way into my life that tilled the soil of my heart in preparation for the help I would find at Didi Hirsch.

About the same time I called Ron, I traveled to Hawaii by myself. I needed time to think and time to renew my love for surfing.

Maybe it was my unaddressed anger at my son's death or a desire to feel in control of something when so much felt out of control. Whatever it was, surfing had become less about enjoyment and finding peace and more about outperforming other surfers. I began to play an internal game of measuring the success of a morning by my position in the lineup of surfers waiting to catch a wave and if I caught the most waves. I did not enjoy the ride as much as I relished beating the guy next to me to the wave. He might be a better surfer than I was, but I was scrappy and could paddle hard. I used this to my advantage to own as many waves as possible.

Surfing in Newport Beach just added to the competitiveness of it all. Most of us who surf there during the week have full-time jobs. We have to get out there early and ride as many waves as possible to make it worth going out before work.

All this combined to take away my joy of surfing. I began to surf less and then barely at all. This robbed me of a place I had always retreated to lay aside what was swirling in my mind and find peace. I needed to recapture what surfing used to mean and what it once gave to me.

I do not know what to call it but the "Aloha Spirit."

It is the ability to surf and have it not be about competition. It is about the joy found in the waves and sharing that joy with others. It is what I went to Hawaii to regain, and I was not disappointed. A week playing in the waters off Oahu and surfing became my happy place again.

When I boarded the plane to fly back home, I brought with me a new perspective on surfing. Maybe it would be better to say a *restored* perspective. I felt like my old self, a person I had not seen or experienced for over three years. This was a person who could actually find joy in life. I was still struggling with grief. I still wanted to fix it all and move forward. But now I had an experience that made me consider that life might bring goodness once again.

At the time I could not have put it that way. All I knew was I could once again go out on the water without picking up the competitive game that had ruined surfing over the past couple of years. I was also able to be alone in my thoughts, without having to chase away the images and questions that had haunted me. Surfing gifted me with peace once again. Those spaces were short-lived, but what mattered most was I could find them for a brief period of time.

I was determined to not lose these renewed perspectives when I got back home. So I began to carve out more time to be alone, and I went back to surfing at my regular spot, this time with the intention of simply finding joy in the pursuit. It was no longer about catching the most waves; it was about the experience of being out there. I even found I had the capacity to enjoy when others caught a great wave. I could share in their joy in ways that I was not able to when I fall into the trap of being competitive. I no longer felt compelled to catch every wave. I just needed my fair share. That was more than enough.

Since I couldn't surf all day, I created other spaces where I could let my mind settle. I would visit the cemetery where my brother is buried. It is a beautiful spot overlooking the ocean, a quiet place where I could allow my mind to clear. Like the ocean, it became a place where I could find peace.

I also created space for my mind to occupy itself with more than business or thoughts about my son's death. I began to read. The fact I made this move would be a shock to those who know me well. I am not one who sits still long enough to read a whole book. In fact, before this I could not tell you the last time I read an entire book. But reading filled my mind with other people's experiences. I could get lost in and inspired by their stories. Reading invited me to consider life and what I might want from it.

My regular conversations with Ron, a rediscovered capacity to enjoy surfing, and the ability to be alone with my thoughts finally led me to a place where I could reach out to the Didi Hirsch clinic.

Ron had suggested that a support group might be helpful, but when I contacted Didi Hirsch, they did not have one starting in the near future, mostly because the entire world was in the grip of the COVID-19 pandemic and still figuring out how to create meaningful connections without actually being in the same place.

This was a big disappointment. It had taken me so long to build up the courage to ask for help, and I was not sure I would still feel so brave in a couple of months. Since jumping right into a group was not possible, I knew I might chicken out if too much time passed. So I pursued individual therapy. Based on my previous disappointing experiences, I had my doubts that counseling now would help much, but I had to do something.

Since Didi Hirsch did not have any support groups to offer at the time, they paired me up with a counselor. If I had doubts about counseling, they were not lessened by the fact this counselor was about the same age as my oldest son and had just graduated from his degree program. It did not feel like I was getting matched up with the sage of grief. But I didn't want to have to start the whole process over, so I gave him a chance. I knew I could always back out if I needed to.

When I met with my counselor, we met on Zoom. It was one of the realities of being in the middle of a pandemic. This actually made it a little easier. I did not feel quite as exposed.

Our first meeting focused on making introductions and setting expectations. Most of our time was spent with me sharing a bit of my life history, talking about what was important to me, and recounting how I had been dealing with the death of my son up to that point. My counselor would need this foundational knowledge in order to accompany me forward. The process felt pretty comfortable and not too heavy. By the time the meeting was over I was thinking, *Okay, that wasn't too bad. I can do this.* It did not hurt that, despite his youth, I liked and connected with my counselor.

In our second meeting, the counselor asked me to begin talking about the death of my son, sharing what had happened. This was difficult. I had been doing my best for three years to avoid talking about these things. I struggled to talk about them to the people I felt closest to and safest with. Now I was being asked to walk through all of it with a stranger. I felt vulnerable and exposed.

While talking about my deepest hurt with someone I did not know seemed totally unnatural, I was surprised to find it very helpful. I could say whatever I was thinking and feeling without worrying about how it would impact the counselor. We would spend our hour together and then I would not see him again for a week. There was a gift in the fact I would not be bumping into him at work or spending the evening with him right after I bared my soul. The separation gave me the ability to risk being completely honest without it affecting the rest of my life.

Of course, it would have an effect on the rest of my life—that was the whole point of going to therapy. At least that is what I hoped. Even though my conversations with Ron had led me to accept that I would always carry my grief, I still was under the illusion that a fix could be found. I knew I could not bring back my son. I knew I could not escape the grief. But I still hoped the time with my counselor would help me fix it ... whatever *it* was.

Over and over again my counselor would tell me that I could not fix it, that I would not be able to return to the life I once knew. As much as I might want to, I could not hit reset and get back to the way things were. It was not possible.

This was a harsh realization he was inviting me to embrace. It should not have been a surprise. Ron had been encouraging me to come to terms with the same thing. Now here was the counselor, making it even more clear. The task at hand was not to fix it, but to learn to live with it. I was frustrated by the fact that this was the way forward and, in my frustration, struggled to accept it. It took time, multiple voices and repeated encouragement for this to finally sink into my head.

It would take me even more time for my heart catch up to what my mind had finally embraced as true.

In the meantime, the counselor kept me talking about the death of my son and how it was impacting my life. It was always hard. It brought feelings up in me that I had spent the better part of three years stuffing. Often, after I would finish a session with my counselor, I would just weep. I could not cry in front of my friends and family, but I would have tears appear in my sessions with my counselor. And when I would turn off the Zoom call when we were finished, I would cry. It still hurt so bad.

While crying was not what I set out to do when I entered counseling, it did help. I would feel relief after the tears had flowed. It was like letting out a deep breath that I had been holding for so long. I would feel lighter, even though nothing had really changed. Feeling was not as bad as I had imagined it would be. I could sit in my sadness and still be okay on the other side. This came as a surprise to me.

Along with my sessions with the counselor, the habit I had created of spending time at my brother's grave gave me additional time during the week to feel my sadness. I could be sad with my counselor, sad after our meeting, and sad all on my own. And I was okay. I was not doing great, but I was okay.

Sadness was not the only emotion the counselor invited me to feel. Anger was another. This felt more dangerous. Anger has lots of energy behind it. It can feel out of control, and if not checked, can unintentionally hurt others. I had tried to put a heavy lid on my anger, but all that did was cause it to seep out sideways. What surfing had become before I made the trip to Hawaii was an example of this. My counselor encouraged me to feel my anger in appropriate ways that did not hurt others or myself.

Sometimes, I just needed to hit something. I would

find myself in the quiet of my car, and the frustration and anger at what Emilio had chosen to do would well up inside of me. I would pound the steering wheel. It did not damage the car, and it did not hurt my hand. But I am sure people next to me at a stoplight or on the freeway might have thought I was crazy or experiencing road rage. It had nothing to do with the road and everything to do with being alone in my car. The quiet space would allow the feelings to rise up and the anger to spill out, without hurting anyone.

Pounding my steering wheel only came at times when my anger snuck up on me. There are more intentional ways to physically express anger, which do no harm to yourself or others. I have heard of people using a swimming pool noodle or baseball bat to hit a bed, or hanging a punching bag in their garage that they can use to unload physical tension. For me, running became an activity where I could let out the tension in my body caused by anger.

It helped that this was something Emilio and I shared, so it was natural for him to come to mind when I ran. Sometimes this would lead me to sadness. The isolation of running by myself made it a safe place to be open. Other times it would lead me to anger. It was easy to pick up the pace and pound the pavement a little harder to allow my body to express the anger I was feeling. Allowing my anger to be appropriately expressed in this way helped me to feel it, dissipating its energy, and helped me get into better shape both mentally and physically.

I was learning that anger, along with all the other feelings, was not something to be avoided. It was a presenting emotion that allowed me to know something else was going on inside of myself. And by being aware of it, I could discover the deeper issue. That was the work the counselor and I were doing. It was not easy for someone like me who had always found a way to stuff his feelings down. Now that I was learning how to feel, I was discovering my emotions were actually good and needed to be experienced if I wanted to move forward.

This gave me the ability to stop spending my energy on avoiding and to begin using it for the task of choosing how I would live moving forward. Conversations with Ron had planted the seeds of this idea; the counselor now encouraged me to make decisions about it. This was a skill I was going to have to learn.

Living is more than going through the motions of life, or even successfully carrying out the responsibilities of all the roles you play. I knew how to be a son, brother, husband, father, friend, and entrepreneur. I gave myself to fulfilling these roles to the best of my ability, but that does not mean I was always actually living when I did so.

When my son died, I continued to press into all these responsibilities, some of them even became a way of escaping the pain. But I would not say I felt like I was living. Surviving? Sure thing. Living? Not so much. My counselor asked me to make decisions that would allow these things to become an expression of life. I had already had a taste of this when I regained my happy place in surfing. I now needed to press that joy and contentment into other areas of my life. Like learning to feel my emotions, this would not be easy for me.

Often, when people are first learning to feel their emotions, it is awkward. Someone who had never learned to express anger without it hurting themselves or others may take some time to learn helpful ways of expression. I had to do that. Making decisions about how to actually live with the death of my son and how to choose life moving forward felt equally awkward. Roles and responsibilities had always set the agenda and paved the way forward. Now I had to learn to make choices about what I wanted and desired in regard to what life would be. I was not particularly good at it.

I have heard you should not make any big life decisions in the first year following the death of a loved one. That first year, I had wanted to sell the house and move. Thankfully, my wife and son kept me from making that decision. But now that I was being invited to choose how to live, the idea came back to me. I started thinking about where I would like to move and what might actually make me happy in a place to live. I began thinking about work and if I really wanted to continue with what I had been doing for the past 30 years. I entertained the idea of retirement. But knowing how much joy I take from creating something new and making it work, I knew I would have to invest my energy somewhere. But where?

I kept thinking choosing would mean change. A change of residence. A change of jobs. A change of responsibilities. I spent several months pondering all the possible changes. It never led me to any answers about what I wanted to do next. The counselor was asking me to make choices about what it would look like to live after the death of my son and I felt stuck trying to come up with the answers, but that did not mean nothing was happening.

In thinking about the possibilities, I started to feel a hopefulness rising up in me. It was something I had not felt since the day the police officers had called me and asked me to meet them at the hospital. I was beginning to believe that there was a life that could be chosen. I began to understand that even though I would never be able to fix it and this grief would never go away or get smaller, I could grow the container of myself to include other things, life-giving things, that would cause the grief to feel lighter.

I was not there yet. But I could at least believe it was actually a possibility, and I was beginning to consider what decisions I might want to make to be able to get there.

During this process, my counselor was also inviting me to care for myself. He asked me to start asking for what I needed and gave me permission to do things that were life-giving. It is nice to have a therapist prescribe surfing as a needed element of self-care.

This was just as hard as the other two areas he had pressed into. I was used to sacrificing to get things accomplished and laying aside my desires to take care of the people I loved. I never considered self-care to be an act of love toward them or a source of the energy needed to fulfill my responsibilities. When first presented with the idea, I thought of it as selfish.

Given this fact, it was not surprising that in trying to learn this new skill, I acted selfishly at first. I made choices about what I wanted and needed that did not take into account all the ways it impacted others. The pendulum had been so far on the side of ignoring my needs that it swung too far back in the other direction. It took time for me to learn how to communicate what I needed and desired, and to be conscious of the impact it was having on others at the same time.

I made space in my life to surf, run, read, and be alone. For the first time, I had time when I was completely by myself for extended periods. I am sure on occasion it felt to Michal as if I were moving away from her. She may even have been afraid of what it might lead to. When the pendulum swung so far to the other side, I have to admit, I wondered as well.

My counselor and Ron kept me grounded and encouraged me to make decisions that would move the pendulum away from the extremes and to the center, a way of being I had never known before.

They guided me in learning to ask for what I needed and desired, prompting me to think about the long-term changes this would create in my life and relationships. They knew joy and happiness would not be found in being able to simply do everything I wanted. It was not about getting all the waves for myself. Joy would be found as I was able to know myself well enough to share it with others. In many ways, I was learning to live the Aloha Spirit I have often returned to Hawaii to recapture. They were inviting me to bring it home, not just to surfing, but to all areas of my life.

Because I had experienced it in my surfing, I was hopeful that a generous, peaceful attitude could one day permeate the rest of my life.

In the end, rather than pulling me away from Michal, these changes gave me the capacity to choose life with her. This felt like a big victory. Now that I was gaining the ability to care for myself and ask for what I needed, I felt that our marriage could not only survive but could ultimately thrive. Whatever life would be discovered after the death of our son, I wanted to discover it with her.

I experienced much growth even while waiting for a support group to form. My time in counseling was more helpful than I anticipated. I grew in my capacity to feel. I accepted at deeper levels the reality that I could not fix the pain and problems. I moved forward in choosing to live amid the grief and heartache. And I was learning to care for myself. This was all new to me. I felt like the training wheels had just been taken off my bike. I was wobbly and a bit erratic, but I was progressing. The fear of falling was being replaced by the excitement of forward motion. I did not have total confidence, but I was beginning to believe I could learn to ride this bike.

All these things came in degrees. Like the swell on the ocean, there is no real way to determine where they began and ended. Yes, there are waves that distinguish themselves from the undulating volume of water that makes up the sea, but while they rise up from it, they are always a part of it. In all that I was learning and growing in, I could not tell you where each lesson definitively began or ended. There were moments, like a wave, where a particular area would rise up and differentiate itself from everything else. But being able to point to a conversation with Ron, session with my counselor, or moment of solitude as the place that gave birth to that area of growth was impossible.

Like surfing, it felt like I was simply responding to the waves that were forming, learning to ride them in response to their unique shape, structure, and power. Maybe more than riding a bike, it seemed like I was learning to surf in an entirely different ocean. I felt like a novice, but I was gaining experience and skill every time I paddled out.

After

CHAPTER EIGHT

Riding On Rails

By the fall of 2020, Didi Hirsch had acclimated to facilitating support groups online and my counselor invited me to join a group that was about to start. I can't say I jumped at the opportunity, but both Ron and my counselor thought it would be helpful and the necessary next step. They were coaching me on how to begin riding bigger and bigger waves. I knew that when it came to navigating grief, I was the novice. I decided to trust them and agreed to join the group even though I did not know what I was really getting into.

I do not know what I expected the group to be like, but I did think that it would be comprised of some, if not all, men. Imagine my surprise when I logged into the Zoom meeting for the first time and found, except for me, the group was made up of all women.

As the women introduced themselves and shared the story of why they were in the group, I realized quickly that everyone else was dealing with a recent death. It had been nearly four years since my son had died.

The other members' emotions were very raw and much more accessible than mine were. I had spent the first three years after my son's death burying my emotions as deeply as possible and avoiding any conversations that might bring them to the surface. Now I found myself in a group of women who had no problem accessing and sharing their pain. The contrast between these women and me made me realize how skilled I had become at avoiding what I felt.

The ease with which these women could "go there" with their feelings made me uncomfortable. Almost immediately, I wondered if I should be in this group. I thought maybe, having taken so long to get into a support group, I had missed the window of opportunity for it to provide the help I needed.

Even though I shared the same life-altering experience with these women, it felt like there was a profound difference between where they were in their grief and where I was four years out from my son's death. My heart ached as I heard their stories. At times their grief seemed overwhelming. I would find myself weeping with them during the session, feeling emotionally spent when our group time was over. I did not know how to hold it or what words to use to offer support. All I could do was listen. And listening was hard.

Of course, when I expressed my doubts about whether I should be in the group, my counselor told me I needed to be. I kept attending, but I am not sure his encouragement was what kept me logging in.

What kept me engaged was the fact that I had heard these women tell their stories. They had invited me into their pain and it felt like I would dishonor them, and the person they lost, if I simply stopped showing up to the group. Because of the trust they had demonstrated by opening their lives, I felt obligated to continue to share in their stories. I often did not know how to respond, but I did know I could be a supportive presence.

This sounds easy, but it is harder than you think. So much can get in the way of simply being present.

As I listened to the other members share, I wrestled with comparison and judgment. No two grief journeys are the same. I had discovered this when seeing how different Michal's experience of grief was from mine. Now I was in a group where not only each member's story was different, but how they processed their grief was equally unique.

There is a temptation to compare the stories, seeing one death as being more tragic than another, or one circumstance as harsher than another. Comparison is an attempt to somehow make yourself feel better about your own circumstance or justify why you are the exception. Neither of these is really helpful, and quite possibly can keep us from doing the work we need to do to move forward. Listening to these women tell their stories taught me that none of us can compare the circumstances and pain of our loss to someone else's.

There was also a temptation to make judgments about how someone was walking through their grief. It is easy to think, *I would have done it this way*. Or, *They should do X, Y, or Z*. Judgment leads us to want to offer advice, and advice is not helpful. We end up presenting ourselves as people seeking to aid or fix, rather than simply being present. There are no easy answers to what moving forward looks like.

I do not know if anyone else was feeling these temptations while in the group, but I had to remind myself not to compare or judge. I had to remember that it is in the listening, being with someone, where the real help is given, both for them and for you. As someone who is used to solving problems and making things work, this was a new skill I was developing while listening to the other group members.

When it came to sharing my own story, I fell silent. Given what these women were sharing about the pain of their loss and how it was impacting their lives, I felt like what I was currently dealing with regarding my son's death paled in comparison. I know it sounds crazy, but somehow I had convinced myself that my story and experience were not worth sharing in light of the intensity of theirs. I felt embarrassed to share what I was currently feeling and dealing with, given how raw they were in the beginning stages of their grief. This is an example of where comparison will lead and how it can keep us from entering in.

Just because I was not sharing didn't mean I wasn't

getting anything from the group. While I felt a bit out of place, I could often hear myself in what other members of the group were sharing. At times, someone put into words exactly what I had been thinking or feeling. These were things I hesitated to talk about with anyone because I thought they would sound crazy. But when I heard someone else share exactly what I had been thinking, I realized I was not crazy. What I had been thinking and feeling was actually quite normal.

Listening to these women not only helped to normalize my experience, but it reinforced that I was not alone, even though it often felt that way. While our stories were not exactly the same, I knew they could relate in ways others could not. These were the first people since the death of my son that I had felt could fully understand what I had gone through and what I had been experiencing ever since. Our group was a place where no explanation was necessary and there was not a need to qualify our statements. We could simply come and be exactly where we were and not be alone.

Discovering what I had been thinking and feeling were normal and that I was not alone came as a huge gift—one I did not realize I needed.

Another surprise to me was how the pain these women expressed became a touchstone for my own grief journey. Before I began the group, I had no real point of reference for the pain I felt. It seemed as if it had just been a constant, never changing in intensity.

Now, being with these women, I could actually see how the pain felt less acute than it had in the beginning. I had not recognized how the container of my life had been expanding to hold the grief. But now I could see clearly that though the grief had not changed, the container was bigger. The grief was not taking up so much space nor was it as heavy. Recognizing the difference in the pain the others were expressing and what I was actually feeling made me feel better about where I was on the journey. I would never "get over" the pain and grief, but I had indeed taken steps toward healing.

While the pain I felt was not as intense as it once was, I was still afraid to put it all out there. During those first few sessions when I felt reluctant to say much, I thought just showing up and listening would be enough. Maybe no one would notice I was not talking much. After all, the rest of the group had so much to share. I was happy for them to fully utilize the limited group time we had available.

Of course, my posture did not go unnoticed by the group's facilitator. Several weeks in a row, he began to encourage me to check in with the group. I stayed quiet, only answering direct questions. During the fourth or fifth week, seeing I was not going to jump in on my own, he began the group by saying, "Let's start with Ed." Of course, he gave me an out, letting me know I only had to speak if I was ready and that I could simply share how my week went. I wish I could say I bared my soul to the group, but I did not. I simply shared how my week had gone, what I was doing for self-care, and some of my current struggles. There was not an outpouring of emotions, but I was at least talking. It was a beginning.

One of the gracious aspects of a group like this is that we could go at our own speed. My counselor would remind me that there was no timeline. I could go at my own pace.

I needed that permission.

Especially helpful with my pace were the reflections other people had written about in regard to the suicide of a loved one, which had been included in the materials distributed to our group. These short articles put words to what I was thinking and feeling. The articles captured people's thoughts and feelings in written form where they could be accessed at any time. I would read these materials over and over again until the words of the authors helped me articulate my own.

One of the quotes from session two's material was from Iris Bolton, a woman who lost her son to suicide and who spent much of her life helping other grieving parents through the books she has authored and her work at The Link Counseling Center in Atlanta, Georgia. She wrote, "Struggle with 'why' it happened until you no longer need to know 'why' or until YOU are satisfied with partial answers." The people in my grief group and people I would never meet who wrote about their experiences helped me to continue to struggle until I no longer needed to know why or I could be satisfied with the partial answers that were available. They were like surf instructors, helping me to learn to ride the wave of my grief, even as they were riding their own.

About the same time that I began meeting in the grief support group, I also began attending a men's Bible study. I was still angry with God, but I knew I needed to try and reconnect with him. If I was ever going to be good with God, it wouldn't happen by remaining distant from him. Reconciliation happens best in proximity. I decided to reach out to another pastor friend and ask if his church had any men's groups I could join. A few weeks later, I was invited to join a new men's group that was forming. I agreed.

In my grief group, I shared little in common with the women, except that we had all lost someone close to us. When I talked about surfing as self-care, I am not sure they fully understood. I hoped this men's group would be different. Still in the COVID protocols of social distancing, we would meet on Zoom. I was excited to see the men who would pop up on the screen when we began meeting.

It turned out we had all been born in 1964, so we naturally called ourselves the Men of '64. But we had more in common than our age and stage of life. I connected with each man in some significant way. There was a fellow restaurateur. A guy who wrestled in high school as I had. One man shared my Chinese heritage. Another shared my Latin American roots. And one father had also lost a child. Many more commonalities emerged as time went on. All of these men made it a group easy to enter into and connect with. It felt like God was giving me a gift in the men who made up this group.

As we began, there was no guarantee this group would lead me to feel any more connected to God, but I felt confident I would end up feeling closer to these men. I was hopeful this would become a place where I could be known and experience a sense of belonging.

The second week into the group, the leader suggested we get to know one another better by creating a timeline of our lives and sharing it with the group. We were all open to the idea and would spend the coming weeks having someone share their timeline each time we met.

Working on my timeline was tough but helpful. I had never sat down to think through the story of my life in chronological order or see the connection between events in separate seasons of my life. In the process of putting my timeline together, I was not only creating something to share with the other men in the group, but I also gained an understanding of my own story. I could see how the way I had navigated my grief, especially in the first few years after the death of my son, had grown from my life story. I could see these threads that had run through my story that influenced how I dealt with problems and where I looked for solutions. These threads had great influence on my life, even though I had not recognized them before I had completed my timeline.

The most influential thread was a sense of abandonment I had carried from a very early age. In the process of immigrating to America, my mother and father were separated by the circumstances that were necessary to bring us to our new homeland. At times, I had to be in one country with my father, while my mother remained in another. It is what they had to do given the situation, but a little kid does not understand the circumstances. All I knew was I wasn't with my mother.

I would not have called it abandonment at the time, nor would my mother have ever thought of it as abandonment. But looking back, that is what it felt like. My response was to become independent, counting on myself to care for my own needs. I learned to deal with life, but I did not learn to feel. Feeling hurt during much of that time, I shoved the feelings down or let them out in the only way I knew how as a kid—through anger.

When Bismarck died, once again I felt abandoned. He was the one who took care of everything and held the family together. We were in the beginning stages of growing our company, my brother had played a significant role in helping us get it launched, and we were still in need of his guidance. While he did not choose to leave us on our own, the tangible outcome was that we could no longer depend on his support. I would have never said he abandoned us, but that is what it felt like. Again, my response was to shove my feelings down so I could deal with my responsibilities.

When Emilio took his life, again it felt like abandonment. Knowing my backstory, it would have been easy to predict how I would respond. I would deal with it by taking care of what needed to be done, but I would not feel it. If I had completed my timeline years earlier, I would have been able to see my patterned response and would have been able to choose a different path. I cannot help but wonder how that might have changed the first three years of life after my son's death.

I was, however, able to see my responses and motivations after completing my timeline. I had to trust this knowledge came at the right moment, when I was finally able to understand it. Now that I was made aware of my patterns of responding to feeling abandoned, and how they had influenced my journey of grief, I was free to make choices about how I would move forward. Before, I really had no choice, my patterns of response were well-worn ruts that kept me heading in the same direction, even if it was not healthy or helpful.

No wonder I had felt stuck and I had found myself continuing to do the very things that lead me to spiral downward.

I was now getting excited about the choices I was able to make. While the ruts had been easy and even comfortable to stay in, I was hopeful that I could start to create a new road that would lead to a greater sense of life.

About the time we were done sharing our timelines, my counselor told me about another grief support group that was forming. This one was going to be all men, and he invited me to participate. I was told there were 15 to 20 men who were interested. I wondered how the group would be different if it were comprised only of men. I knew how helpful my men's Bible study group had been and I hoped this would be the same. I agreed to participate.

By the time the group actually began, only three of us showed up. This was disappointing, but unfortunately, very typical for men. Men just do not believe that a group like this will be of help, or they are afraid that attending such a group will cause all kinds of uncomfortable feelings to spill out. I understand those fears, but because I had seen how helpful a group experience could be, I was really hoping more men would take the risk of participating.

Because there were only three of us, I knew there would be no hiding in this group. There would be plenty of time for all of us to share. This was scary, but I was not going to turn back now.

It was easier to talk this time around, not just because the group was only men, but also because I had been working through significant issues for the past six months and had become more comfortable opening up. I listened to the other men share their stories and talk about how they were handling the death of their child. As I listened, I realized I was not in the same place as they were. I would sometimes catch myself speaking as someone who was a little further along on the path. Often my reflections on what they shared were encouragements born out of experience. I might not be able to show them what the destination looked like, but I was learning to help them see the next step. I may have not been the best person to talk about how to navigate grief. I was definitely not a pro surfer when it comes to riding this wave. But I was discovering that I actually had something helpful to share. This came as a surprise to me and felt in a small way like something was being redeemed in the middle of the loss.

Once again, a mirror was held up to me that allowed me to see that the container had continued to grow, even though I had not noticed it was expanding. This made me feel good. When the destination feels so far away, these small realizations of movement give us a sense of hope. Could it even be possible to feel hope, even after the death of a child? I was discovering that hopefulness could indeed happen.

If my old patterns felt like being stuck in a rut, counseling and involvement in groups felt like rails I could ride that would help me break free from the ruts. Since the ruts were formed in childhood by an unconscious response to the feeling of being abandoned, these rails were leading me to make conscious choices about the way to respond in the future. These would involve basic choices about things like spirituality, marriage, work, feelings, self-care, serving others, gratitude, and how I would carry my son's memory forward with me.

I never imagined having to make some of these choices. But rather than feeling overwhelmed by them, I now felt like I had the ability to choose. I did not have to be stuck in a rut any longer. I could pave a new road forward. The choices I would make would determine just what kind of road that would be. I would not be simply choosing life—I would be choosing how I desired to live.

This felt like forward movement and more evidence that the container was growing.

CHAPTER NINE

Forward Motion

You do not have to be a surfer to understand the physical strength and agility required for the sport. Paddling out through the breaking waves, positioning yourself in the set, digging to catch a wave, then popping up off of your board and placing your feet on the deck so you can carve through the waves all require the physical engagement of your body.

But ask skilled surfers and they would tell you much more is required. Surfing also demands the engagement of the mind as you are judging the swells and picking out where to position yourself to catch the best waves. There is something about the concentration and focus needed for the sport that helps you to set aside all that is filling your thoughts and just be present. Surfing clears and calms the mind.

Surfing also impacts your emotions. You can find yourself on a high after you have just ridden a wave and gotten everything out of it that it had to offer. And you can find yourself frustrated because you just missed dropping in on a great wave, or got cut off by another surfer. There are good waves and bad waves, good days and bad days, and you feel it all.

While surfing seems like an individual sport—it is just you, your board, and the waves—in reality it is relational. Many of my closest friendships have formed because of my involvement in surfing. The relationships formed on the beach and waves become a brotherhood. We support, understand, and enjoy one another, even if at times we also compete with one another.

Surfing touches you spiritually. Yes, it is a sport, but being on the ocean, feeling the swells beneath you, looking out from the shore to the great expanse of the sea and sky can also make you feel like it is a holy endeavor, connecting you to creation and the Creator. Those who surf go out for the thrill of the ride, but they also go out because the ocean offers a spiritual experience. It is sacred space—at least that is how it often feels to me.

Surfing impacts every part of you; physically, mentally, emotionally, spiritually, and relationally. And so does grief.

You do not need to experience the death of a child, or some other significant person in your life, to understand the impact grief has on you emotionally. The pain and sadness that it brings are not a surprise to anyone. What is a surprise to many is how the death of a loved one also impacts them physically, mentally, relationally, and spiritually.

The previous chapters were filled with examples of

how the impact of my son's death affected every part of me. Physically, I struggled to sleep. Mentally, I found it hard to focus and my mind kept wrestling with the why questions anytime it got quiet. Emotionally, I was sad, angry, and drained. Relationally, I withdrew. Spiritually, I felt disappointed with God and did not know if I could trust him.

These examples just touch the surface of how the death of my son impacted the different parts of me.

I wish I could say the work we did in the support group and the issues we were exploring in my men's group brought all these things back to center. They did not. But what they did do was make me aware of ways in which I needed to be gracious to myself and ways in which I needed to care for myself.

I needed to offer myself grace to recognize that what I experienced was normal. The fact that so many aspects of my life were impacted was not a sign of weakness. It was a sign I am human. Given I was human and this was normal, I could then care for myself in specific ways that address each of these areas. This knowledge allowed me to advocate for myself, which would in turn give me the capacity to make choices about what moving forward would look like.

Physically, I cared for myself by surfing, running, going to the gym, and getting enough sleep. Grief produced a lot of energy in my body. I needed a place where it could be worked out, literally. Of course, the temptation is to do nothing. We don't feel like doing anything. It might have been more appealing to just sit on the couch and not engage the body in any activity, but the reality was I would sleep better if I worked out. My anger would have less energy if I had run hard. And the endorphins released by the physical exertion would impact my mood and mental state.

Along with working out, I began to carefully consider what I drank, for reasons made obvious in the previous chapters. And I also started to watch what I was eating. I wanted food to be a way I fueled my body or enjoyed life, not a way I dealt with my emotions. As I ate better, I also felt better. It is amazing how all these things are interconnected.

Mentally, self-care meant making space for myself where I could focus on something other than the unanswered questions or the images of my son's death that often haunted me. The habit of reading allowed me to absorb other people's thoughts and experiences. At times, I would find myself at the end of a page, not being able to recall a word that was written there. But the printed page allowed me to back up, refocus, and read the words again.

This practice of focusing my thoughts elsewhere—and I mean *practice* because it did not come naturally to me—gave my mind the break it needed and continues to need. Reading is not an escape from the reality of the death of my son and how it continues to impact our family. It is more like the space between sets of waves that allows you to recover and regroup in order to make yourself ready to catch the next wave. Like a muscle needs rest to allow the work of weight training to produce strength, reading provided my mind the rest it needed to gain the strength to integrate my son's death and continue to live.

Emotionally, I cared for myself by finding places like my support group that would encourage me to feel. I would also take time to journal about what I was feeling in the moment, as well as the good memories I shared with my son. There are many of those, and I was emotionally better off if I could hold on to the beautiful memories of his life.

I did not always know what I felt, but I could discover my inner world by talking about what I was feeling with others or contemplating my feelings when I was alone. The emotions I was most afraid to feel would lose their power when they were spoken out loud or written down on paper.

Most of us think of emotions as being good or bad. As I have learned to recognize and express my emotions, I've discovered that they are simply an indication of what is going on in my heart. Being able to see that reality is always a good thing.

Another way I cared for myself emotionally was allowing myself to enjoy little things. At first, I wondered how I could enjoy anything when my son had died. But eventually I realized that savoring small pleasures did not dishonor my grief process and did not dishonor my son's memory. I found little things like treating myself to a café latte and drinking it slowly, savoring a piece of chocolate, allowing myself to delight in the beauty of the ocean, or settling into the Aloha Spirit to feed my sense of joy. This too took practice. I had to press past my feelings of guilt about enjoying something and embrace the fact that I could hold both joy and sorrow. This is part of what it means to be emotionally mature, and it is necessary for emotional health.

Relationally, I continued to open up—not to everyone but to people I had discovered could walk this journey with me. I continued to talk with Ron and made it a priority to meet with my men's group each week. I also made plans with friends to do things we enjoyed like dining out, surfing, and traveling. The loss of my son had led me to feel very alone and isolated. I might not always be able to control the way I feel, but I can make choices about the time I spend with people and how open I am with my life. There is still work to do here, but when the opportunity presents itself, I am choosing to press into relationships.

Spiritually, I care for myself by being involved in a Bible study where we can bring our unanswered questions about God and explore what it means to trust him. I have read books that have explored who God is and what we can know about him. I continued to press into prayer and open my heart to God, even when all my heart wants to say is "I don't trust you."

The death of my son made me question many things about who God is and how he works. But it also caused me to realize that I need the hope that is made possible through his love and the promise that this life is not all there is.

It is still a journey, but I am caring for myself on that journey by engaging with people and spiritual practices that help me move forward. I will never have all the answers, but I am growing in the faith necessary to trust in the areas that remain unclear and probably always will be. I am diligently seeking, and that is a good thing for my soul.

All of this self-care awakened me to the reality that there really was life possible after the loss of a child. It would not be the life I had always imagined. It would not be the life I would have chosen, but there was a life I could choose. It would be different, but it could also be good. It would certainly contain sorrow, but it could also hold the joy of many things. I knew my son would want me to take hold of that joy. I also knew I needed to take hold of it, not just for me, but for the son still with me, for my wife, for my extended family, and for the many people who make up what has been and is a really rich life.

A quote from the movie *The Shawshank Redemption* says, "Get busy living or get busy dying." I knew there was only one choice worth making. I had been invited to choose life, and I was regaining the ability to make decisions about what that life would look like. It was time to get busy living.

This was a change in perspective for me. When I first started meeting with my counselor I would say, "The seventeen and a half years I had both of my sons were the best years of my life." I truly thought I had lived the best years of life as their father. The death of my youngest son had stripped the completeness and goodness of that from me, and now the years ahead felt like they were destined to be a sorry second best. My counselor challenged this thinking. He invited me to consider that there were good years ahead, maybe even some of my best.

At first, I thought he was crazy. There was no possible way that could be right. But as time went on, I came to wonder if he might be correct. Learning to care for myself, developing the capacity to hold both joy and sorrow, embracing the reality that good years ahead would not erase the good years behind with my son, allowed me to begin to envision the possibility that the best really could be yet to come. This led me to specific choices that would order my life and open me to the promise of future goodness.

The first choice I made was to choose my wife. When we stood before one another on our wedding day, we made vows to one another that included "for better or worse." We now knew how bad *worse* could actually be, but we also knew how great *good* could be. I wanted to honor my vows, not by just staying married, but by living in the reality of the worse and pressing toward the life found in the good.

To the outside world, there may have been no

perceivable difference, but I knew in my heart what I was doing all over again was choosing her. On our wedding day, we declared that choice before our family, friends, and God with great hope. All these years later, after weathering this hardship together, I was not simply choosing to stay married. I was choosing her with hope for the good life we could still create and live together.

I also made the choice of being a father to the son who remained. He had my heart, but having dealt with my grief in the first few years by filling my days with work and my evenings with numbing, that reality had not always been demonstrated clearly. I wanted him to experience fully that he is not only loved but also pursued by his father. I began to reach out to talk and made time to do the things we enjoy. I wanted to make new memories, creating new experiences of joy. I wanted to listen as he talked about his plans for the future. I wanted to hear his dreams and encourage him to press toward them. And I wanted to offer the kind of help and support a father can give.

He was walking through his own journey of grief. I knew it had been hard on him, and I wanted to give him a place where he could talk about it when he was ready. And when the time was right, I desired to tell him what I was learning. I might be only a step or two ahead of him on the path, but I wanted to share with him what I was discovering and applying to my life to help him avoid some of the pits I had fallen into along the way.

The choices I would end up making about how I desired to live were not only about relationships. One of the realities that my son's death awakened me to was that life is shorter than we realize, and the ability to share it with others in the way we imagine is not guaranteed. I felt older after having walked through the past five years. Physically, I was in better shape than I had been in years, but my soul felt like it had endured more years than the calendar would indicate. I was awakened to the fact that time is precious, and I wanted to spend it with people I loved and doing things we enjoyed.

I began to invite Michal to dream about the places we wanted to travel and the things we wanted to do. I was really inviting both of us to begin to imagine living into the future. This was so important. By imagining the future, we were not allowing the loss of our son to keep us from living.

Having already taken some of these trips that Michal had planned, I can tell you they were not completely free from grief. Emilio was—and is—always with us. We might be eating at a place we know he would enjoy or doing something that would be right up his alley, and we are reminded that he would love it. We are also reminded he is not there. This brings sadness, but it also surprisingly brings some hints of joy as well. While he is not there physically, he is with us in a very tangible way.

It is like this in so many things we do, whether we

are on a trip or living in the regular rhythm of life back at home. The seventeen and a half years we enjoyed with our son—who he was, how he responded to life, and the memories we shared—all continue to accompany us as we move forward. In choosing to live, find joy in life, and make new memories, we are not leaving Emilio behind. We take him with us. And while I would much rather have him fully here, I am so grateful he is still present in our hearts and minds. His life continues to bring joy to ours.

As I began to make choices about what it would look like to live life, I also began to rethink what I wanted my work life to become.

Before my son died, I was already in a transition of moving from being a builder of businesses to a mentor of those who were learning to build. That did not keep me from birthing new businesses. In the years since Emilio's death, I had started two new restaurants and a doughnut shop, with more locations in the works.

These had a different goal than the businesses I had begun when I was young. When I was starting out, it was all about money, growth, and success. Now I was envisioning, along with my partners, businesses that gave back. We wanted to leverage success to help others. The new businesses we formed all had a component of serving others, whether it was offering them an opportunity to develop the skills necessary to build a life's work or partnering with organizations to raise support for the good work they were doing.

In the beginning of my grief, some of these new endeavors gave me a reason to get out of bed. I needed the purpose and responsibility to pull me forward, but I have learned not to allow them to become a way of escaping the grief itself. They still give purpose, but rather than being a place to hide, they have become a place of life, a place where I can invest in impacting the lives of others. It is the kind of work that creates a sense of gladness and joy.

Work and success will be measured differently over the next ten years. That excites me. A couple of years ago, I could not imagine being excited about anything. But as the container of my life has grown, as I have learned to hold both joy and sorrow at the same time, I have discovered it is possible to be excited again and give myself to work and activities that are life-giving.

Along with missing my son, I also often think about how he would want us to move forward in light of what happened. He would want us to be happy. He would want us to remember him with love and fondness. He would not want that one moment to be the one thing that defined his life or ours. Knowing these things, I feel like in making the choice to live and enjoy life, I am choosing to honor him. I honored him when we celebrated his birth with our friends and family. There were many ways in his seventeen and a half years of life that we honored who he was and what he accomplished. We honored him at his death, when friends and family gathered to celebrate his life and its impact on all of us. And we continue to honor him by choosing to live a life that has been influenced by him and that carries the influence forward.

Grief will always be our companion. It not only reminds us that he is not here, but it also reminds us of how dearly we loved him. While in the beginning I would have done anything to escape the pain of the loss, I now realize it will always be connected to the joy of Emilio being my son and the enjoyment of who he was and the life we shared.

This is where my journey of grief has brought me. I needed mentors along the way to help me quit diving under the waves and learn to navigate them instead. To find these people, I had to risk reaching out for help. In doing so, I found that I was not alone. There were others who could be with me and there were others who could understand. They helped me stop avoiding, numbing, and hiding. They taught me to be present to the part of my heart that was broken.

If you have ever tried to stand up on what surfers call a shortboard on a flat ocean, you know how important forward motion is. It is nearly impossible to keep your balance and the board will not hold your full weight above the surface of the water. For someone who has spent their whole life surfing, it might be possible to stay upright on a shortboard when there are no waves for a few seconds, maybe even a few minutes. But everyone will eventually be overtaken by the instability and lack of buoyancy of the board and fall.

But if there are waves and you are able to paddle and catch one, dropping in and popping up, you will know what it is like to harness its energy into forward motion. The unstable board suddenly becomes something you can stand on. Moments earlier you may have been struggling with the board just to keep your balance as you sat on it, waiting for a wave. Adding the forward motion creates stability and allows you to ride the board across the face of the wave. It is then you can participate with the wave, carving and cutting your way through it. In that moment, you find yourself immersed in the joy of surfing.

In surfing, when you fall off your board, they call it a wipeout. When you get spun about so violently under the water after falling off your board that you lose control of your body, they call it being *ragdolled*. You literally are tossed by the wave like a ragdoll.

My son's death had ragdolled me. It changed me forever. It took time for me to recover, but the forward motion I found was allowing me to stand up once again and ride life's waves. I rediscovered that forward motion could bring stability, invite participation, and give birth to moments where I could actually be immersed in joy.

I know my son would want these things for his family and friends.

I wish he were here to share the joy of riding the

waves with us.
   I will always wish that.

After

CHAPTER TEN

Emilio's Life

Every now and again, some of Emilio's close friends come into the restaurant for a meal. They make a point of doing so when they are in town. I think they want to check in with us, and it is always great to see them. Michal often takes time to chat with them and catch up on life. She then passes the news on to me. Their conversations generally have two threads. The first is all about catching up. They are all about to graduate college. Michal talks with them about how that feels and what their plans are now that they are about to pass this important milestone.

Some of their plans are immediate. The last time they stopped by, a group of them were planning to take a trip the following weekend. This was a tradition they had begun when they were in high school. Back then Emilio would have been right in the middle of deciding where they would go and what they would do. It did my heart good to hear they were still taking these trips, even though it pointed to the fact my son would not be with them.

Other plans are more long term. When they talk to

Michal, they always bring her up to speed on their hopes for their further education and what they are thinking about in regard to their careers. Two are headed to medical school. I am excited for them.

The other thread of conversation is made up of memories. They are not afraid to talk about Emilio, the memories they made with him, and the ways he influenced their lives.

Of course, I think about him every day. And it is good for my soul to know there are others who think about him often as well. While he is physically not present, the way he impacted their lives continues to shape who they are becoming.

An example of this is exemplified by one of these friends. Back in high school, this boy was not very interested in school, and I am pretty sure he did not give much thought to college. For whatever reason, he did not have the desire, or maybe he did not think he had the ability, to go to college. Emilio refused to let him settle for anything less than keeping all his options open and pushed him to take his studies seriously.

Emilio encouraged and prodded him to do his best. I am sure there were times Emilio seemed like a nudge, but all that nudging accomplished its intended effect, as the young man is about to graduate college.

Emilio would be very pleased.

This reminded me of another story from Emilio's high school experience. He had a friend who had suffered from a physical issue that led to a hospital stay and then ongoing cognitive impairment that took a while to overcome. I would imagine for many high school boys, this kind of condition would have made them uncomfortable and they might have found excuses to make themselves scarce. Not Emilio. He chose to press into the friendship.

When his friend was in the hospital, Emilio would often go visit this friend, seeking to cheer him up. Once, he even showed up in a chicken costume. To this day, a smile comes to my face when I think about him walking through the hospital dressed like a chicken looking for his friend's room. Most of us would be too embarrassed to do that, but not Emilio. If it would raise the spirits of a friend and make them forget what they were dealing with for a few moments, he was all in.

When his friend returned to school, he had trouble remembering where his classes were. Emilio stepped in to be his personal guide. He would make sure his friend got to class before he made his way to his own. This made him late, but his teachers understood and gave him a pass. They also allowed him to leave early so he could be waiting for his friend when class was over to help him find the next room.

While this was a unique case, other friends could tell stories about how Emilio reached out to encourage and include them. He saw people who were on the outside of the circle and was always pulling them toward the center. He was thoughtful, tenderhearted and loving.

When he was graduating from junior high school, Emilio told me that he wanted to get a group of friends together to go paddle boarding as a way to celebrate. He wanted to know if he could use my board. My parents live on Balboa Island, which is where I keep my board. I told him I would be happy to go with him and carry the board to the water for him and get him all set up. He resisted, insisting he could do it himself.

The board was much bigger than Emilio was, and I knew he would struggle to get it from the house to the ocean without dinging it up. So I told him I would help him get to the water and then make myself scarce. I would go running around the island while he and his friends did their thing.

We got to the water's edge before anyone else arrived. I got Emilio settled and then took off running. Because I ran around the perimeter of the island, I eventually made my way back to where he was. I was surprised at what I saw: rather than a group of friends, there was just Emilio paddling the board with a girl sitting on the front of it, facing him. They were engaged in conversation. I knew in an instant that this was not a celebration of graduation—it was a date. My son, in typical fashion, had planned a thoughtful way to spend the afternoon with a girl he liked.

I did not interrupt them and did not call attention to the fact I was passing by. I just smiled and thought,

That's my boy.

Later, when I went to help him take the board back to my parents' house, I asked him what happened to all his friends. He smiled and said something about them not being able to come, but I am pretty sure he knew that I understood it had been a date all along.

While he might have been embarrassed to admit it to his dad, he did demonstrate a lot of confidence in asking the girl to go paddle boarding. He had worked hard to gain this confidence.

When Emilio was in fifth grade, his friends were all on the track team. He decided he wanted to participate as well. When he went to the coach to express his interest, Emilio was told no. He had asthma and was a bit overweight. I can see why the coach might have thought he wasn't the best fit for the track team. But as a father, I hoped the coach would have had more optimism about Emilio's ability to improve and grow.

My heart was broken by Emilio's disappointment. I knew if he set his mind to something, he would make it happen. He would make the commitment and investment to become a valuable member of the team. I talked to the coach about the situation, but it did not change his decision.

Then came the Irvine track and field championship, an event in which anyone could compete. I told Emilio that if he wanted to run, I would help him train. He was all in.

For four months we trained five days a week. He

worked hard. His body began to change, and he improved his speed. But more importantly, at a season of life when many kids are pulling away from their parents, we became super close.

When the meet rolled around he competed in the 50- and 400-meter events. He won the 50 and took third in the 400. He was the only kid from his school to medal. I was thrilled for him and proud of how disciplined he had been at working toward his goal. I was thankful I had been able to share the whole experience with him. If the coach had let him on the team, I might never have had the opportunity to be a part of Emilio's training and preparations.

After he received his medals he walked off the field, past the coach and the principal of his school, and came directly over to me to show me his medals. It was a moment of joy and celebration. He had not given up when others did not think he could do it. He had achieved his goal.

For the next year, we continued training. I loved the time it created for us to spend together. When the championships rolled around again, he ran the same races. This time he came in first in the 400 and third in the 50. He became an amazing 400-meter runner.

The bond we formed in that season of training for the championships would carry through the rest of his life. Training and running together became our thing. We worked out together two to three times a week. No matter how busy life got, we always had on our calendar time to train. It kept us connected.

Emilio's Life

When I run now, he is always with me.

When the boys were young, I was the one who drove them to school each morning. It was always a nice touchpoint at the beginning of the day. When Emilio was just six years old, believe it or not, we would talk about the stock market on the way to school. We would listen to the morning market report, and he would ask questions about it. After a time, he began to initiate the conversation, asking how the market was doing. He probably had the best understanding of the stock market that you could expect a six-year-old to have. He would ask me, "How is our money today?" I would reply, "The market is up today, so Daddy's stocks are doing well."

I realized the subject was way over his head, but I also knew he was interested in it because he knew I was. Emilio was like that. From an early age, he was interested in what other people found important and was willing to enter their world. Our conversations about stocks on the way to school were this part of who he was.

When we would get to school, he would take my hand and I would walk him to the classroom. Some mornings, we would arrive before the teacher. The door would be locked and I would find a spot against the wall and sit down to wait. Emilio would crawl up into my lap, and we would then talk about things that were important to him. We would talk about school, his friends, or whatever it was that was of interest to him at the moment. I don't remember all we talked about, but I do remember the feeling of sitting there with him on my lap, content to wait for the teacher, because we could fill the space with simply being together. It was an opportunity for me to enter into his world, and I cherished being invited to do so.

One day, we arrived and found the door locked. I went to sit down and he told me to stand back up. I was surprised by this. He seemed embarrassed. I wondered if that precious season had come to an end. My heart sank a little.

Come to find out, it had nothing to do with being embarrassed about being with Dad and everything to do with the crush he had on a girl. He did not want to be perceived as a little boy who crawled onto his father's lap; he wanted her to see him as a potential boyfriend. He was six going on sixteen. It was fun to share that with him as well, even though I did not make much of it.

He eventually convinced his mom into inviting the little girl over for a play date. As evidenced by his experience with running track, when Emilio set his mind to something, he was determined to see it through.

I could fill pages with stories like these, some of them significant milestones, others fleeting moments that captured a bit of who Emilio was. He had a kind and tender heart, but he was also determined and willing to do the hard work to achieve what he desired. He saw people and included them, and often was the instigator of the plans his friends made together. He could be bossy, but it was always motivated by a vision of what they could do or experience together.

It is always good to remember these things. I have included a taste of who he was here because I don't want to leave you with only the memory of his death, but also with the memory of a sweet little boy, who was growing into a man who had significant impact and influence on the lives of his friends and family. Our lives were richer, more enjoyable, and more meaningful because we shared life with him.

When I have moments like the one I shared with his friends when they came into the restaurant, I am reminded how the influence of his life continues to reverberate in the lives of others. I know the trajectory of their lives has been shaped in part because they knew him and his ability to believe in and encourage people.

When I hear them talk about continuing to do things they used to do with him, I know they too are carrying him forward. He might not always be on their minds and in their thoughts, but he is also not far from it. It gives me joy to think, as they are making new memories, they are recalling how those are built on the memories they made with my son.

For me personally, I often think about how Emilio would respond in a situation. I find that his example of determination helps me to be more determined in moments when it would be easy to give up. I draw inspiration to press on when I'm tempted to believe someone else's estimation of what I am able to accomplish.

When I might be prone to not see someone, I am reminded of Emilio's capacity to see and include others. So much of the focus of my work now is built upon finding ways to encourage and help others. That capacity is something I saw in and learned from my son.

I might have taught him about money, but his life taught me something much more important.

Every time those of us who knew Emilio meet someone where they are, care for them, and invite them into the circle, they are being influenced by my son. They'll never meet him, of course, but they will be influenced in a very tangible way.

This doesn't mean the sadness has gone away.

Part of my heart still breaks when I am reminded he is not there. I think others instinctively know this and so they have a tendency to not speak about Emilio's life. They refrain from sharing memories or discussing the last time he popped into their mind in the middle of the day. They don't talk about ways they see his life continue to impact theirs, for fear talking about it will just press on the wound, causing more pain.

I am thankful his friends have not been constrained by that fear. I am always grateful when they make time to come by and chat with Michal, sharing their lives and including Emilio in the conversations. It makes it possible for the sadness to be accompanied by the continuing discovery of ways he is still present—not only in memories from the past, but also through the ways those who knew him continue to live in light of the influence he had on our lives.

This knowledge is the best gift you can give to a parent who has lost a child. We need to know that their life mattered and that the influence of their being here continues to ripple through the lives of others.

Because I am a person of faith, I believe that one day I will see my son again. In that moment, the sadness will finally be washed away. Scripture says there will be no more death or tears or pain. All that will remain is life and joy.

I long for that day with my whole heart.

Until then, I will hold on to this promise of hope, and I will carry my son forward with me, allowing his life and example to continue to strengthen and encourage mine.

I will also always carry the wound of his death. I do not have a choice in the matter. Emilio's death has changed me. And like someone who has suffered a debilitating injury–because that is what the loss of a child is–my task is to continue to learn to live with the reality of my son's death, overcoming the injury it has caused, and endeavoring to live the best life possible.

This is what it means to integrate the death of my son.

I may not be able to bring my son back, but I can

give myself to integrating his life and his death into mine.

This is the only way forward I know.

APPENDIX ONE

Dos And Don'ts

If you would have come to me before my son's death and asked for advice on how to help a friend whose child had died, I would have told you I had no idea. In a culture where we do everything we can to avoid the pain of death, we are not trained on how to walk with others in these hard places. Unless you are a trained professional, it seems you only come to understand what is needed or how to comfort others by enduring the loss of a loved one yourself.

What follows is what I have learned from the experience of my son's death that might be of help. I say *might* because everyone's journey through grief is different. I would encourage you to hold the lists that follow like points on a compass–they will point you in the right direction, but they will not give you every detail of the path.

If you are the one whose child has died, allow these lists to help you identify what you need, but give yourself permission to see them only as a starting point. Recognize that over time what is needed will change. What is helpful at the beginning may be totally unhelpful later on. Do not be afraid to change what you ask for when people offer their help and support, and realize this may be the case when you are coming alongside a friend who is grieving.

What follows are not exhaustive lists, but they do provide a place to begin.

For the Friend

Don't try to fix it. The tragedy and the aftermath of grief cannot be fixed. It is broken. The journey of grief is not to try and get back to how things were before, but to recognize that they have forever been altered. You must learn to live in this new normal. Trying to fix it just delays the process.

Don't try to say something that will make it better. When people who have experienced the death of a loved one get together, a topic that often comes up is the well-meaning but stupid things people say. These things are not said because people want to be hurtful. They are said in an attempt to make it feel better. It would be far better to say nothing, or to simply acknowledge how painful it is, than try to say something to take away the pain. Phrases like "He is in a better place" may be true, but they do not diminish the pain, especially in the beginning.

Do listen. This is probably the best way you can help. In listening, you communicate you are with the person. You allow them to feel what they are feeling and let them know they are not alone. Some of what you hear may be uncomfortable. Don't be afraid to sit in the discomfort. In speaking thoughts and feelings out loud, they lose some of their power. Giving a grieving person the space to speak and be heard helps them move through their grief in ways you may not understand in the moment.

Don't ask what someone needs and assume they will be able to tell you. The truth is the person in grief, especially at the beginning, may not know what they need.

Do think about what would be helpful and be willing to take the initiative. Offer to take care of tasks they have no capacity to think about doing. Bring a meal. Offer to take their children to soccer practice. Buy groceries and drop them off. Ask if you could clean the house or mow the lawn. They may not realize what a gift it is in the moment, but later on they will look back and realize those unsolicited acts of kindness helped to carry them through.

Do try to do these things as unobtrusively as possible. For example, if you are dropping a meal off, do not plan on staying for a long conversation. If they want to talk and invite you in, be available. But if they keep the conversation short and send you on your way, do not be offended. Give them the gift of space along with the meal.

Do everything tentatively. You might ask, "Would it be helpful if I picked up the kids from school?" They might say, "That's great!" Or, "Actually, I want to pick them up, but it would be helpful if you could swing by the grocery story and grab some milk. I just don't have it in me to go shopping." Either way, you are serving in the way that would feel most helpful to them. The same thing works for asking questions about what they are thinking or feeling. Offering the questions tentatively invites reflection and response, rather than a simple yes or no answer. This is important as they are discovering what they think, feel and need.

Do continue to reach out long after the memorial service. It gets very quiet after the celebration of life is complete and all of the friends and family get back to their normal rhythms of life. Make it a habit to check in regularly. Set a reminder on your phone, if that is helpful. Make calls, send texts, and drop a handwritten note in the mail. Just letting them know you are thinking about them is great. Telling stories about the person who died and sharing how they impacted your life is even better. Parents love to hear others fondly remember their child. Unfortunately, people stop talking about the person who died, in part because they are afraid it will cause pain. The most painful thing is when no speaks their name.

For the One Experiencing Grief and Loss

Do advocate for what you need. You may struggle to even know what that might be, but when you do discover it, do not be afraid to ask for it.

Do find ways to care for yourself. You need those moments of self-care to sustain you. Make a list of things that help and return to that list when you

Appendix 1

begin to feel like it is all too much. Pick something you can give yourself permission to do, like taking a walk, listening to calming music, or getting a massage. Search the internet for self-care ideas and note the ones that feel like they would be of help to you.

Do find time to journal what you are thinking and feeling. You may not even know what to write when you sit down, but the process of journaling will help you discover what you are thinking and feeling. Being able to recognize and acknowledge these things are important in grief. Do not worry about being eloquent. Just be honest. No one ever needs to read these pages, so pour out all that is inside.

Do identify the people you can depend upon for support. The more people on this list the better. These are the people you can call upon at any time, who will be able to provide a listening ear or a helpful hand. Know who is good at what. Not every support person can meet every kind of need. Some can sit with you as you weep. Know who they are and call them when that is what is necessary. Some are the kind of people who can get things done and they find joy in the task. Know who they are and call them when needed.

Don't use substances or work to hide from or numb the pain. This will not make the hurt and pain go away. It just compresses it, gives it more energy, and makes it more destructive. It also prolongs and multiplies it. If this is a temptation for you, find someone you trust to talk with about it and give them permission to ask you how you are doing in this area.

Do reach out for support from people and organizations that understand grief. Dealing with a death of a loved one is not something anyone wants to go through, but it is something we will all have to face. There are people who understand what it takes to get through it. You don't have to figure it out on your own. Tap into their experience and expertise. Appendix Two has some places you might begin to look for this kind of support.

Do give yourself grace. Dealing with the death of your child is hard. It is the hardest thing you will ever have to do. You don't have to do it perfectly. Allow for mistakes. Know you will make them, and learn from them. When you do make one, forgive yourself. It does yourself no good to add guilt to the pile of grief you are already having to endure. Movement, not perfection, is the way to measure forward motion.

APPENDIX TWO

Recommended Resources

Organizations

Here are some resources that may aid in your quest to find people who can walk alongside of you. Not every one of them may be a perfect fit. Do not be afraid to reach out and explore if the organization feels like a good fit for you. You may need to connect with one or two of them before you find the right one.

Didi Hirsch Mental Health Services. This is a model organization offering suicide prevention and mental health services. They have a comprehensive array of crisis services, therapy, support, and training. You can find out more at: www.didihirsch.org.

Pathways. Centered in south Los Angeles County, this organization provides grief support to people who have experienced the death of a loved one. They offer free bereavement groups for students, adults, and families. Find them at: www.pathwayshospice.org.

The Dougy Center. This organization's mission is to provide grief support in a safe place where children, teens, young adults, and their families can share their experiences before and after a death. They create safe places to share and connect with others who understand what you are going through. For more information go to: www.dougy.org.

The Compassionate Friends. Focusing on families who have lost children, this organization provides highly personal comfort, hope, and support to every family experiencing the death of a son or a daughter, a brother or a sister, or a grandchild, and help others better assist the grieving family. They are on the web at: www.compassionatefriends.org.

Grief Share. This organization offers weekly faith-based support groups for people who have lost a spouse, child, family member, or friend. Each session includes a video seminar led by an expert in grief, focused group discussion and personal study and reflection. You can find out more at: www.griefshare.org.

Appendix 2

Books

I offer these books because I know some people may prefer to begin with something to read rather than jump right into a support group. I encourage you to find a group of people to meet with even as you receive help from books you read. There is something powerful about working through your grief in community. A book cannot fully replace that. Still, these books come highly recommended and are worth looking into.

A Grace Disguised, Revised and Expanded: How the Soul Grows through Loss, Jerry L. Sittser (Zondervan, 2021). With vulnerability and honesty, Jerry Sittser walks through his own grief and loss to show that new life is possible—one marked by spiritual depth, joy, compassion, and a deeper appreciation of simple and ordinary gifts.

Experiencing Grief and Loss, H. Norman Wright (B&H Books, 2003). This is a brief but profound book written for those who find themselves in the wake of the despair grief leaves.

I Wasn't Ready to Say Goodbye: Surviving, Coping and Healing After the Sudden Death of a Loved One, Brook Noel (Sourcebooks, 2008). Whether you're grieving the sudden loss of a loved one or helping someone else through their grief, this book offers a comforting hand to help guide you through the grieving process, from the first few weeks to the long-term emotional and physical effects.

It's OK That You're Not OK: Meeting Grief and Loss in a Culture That Doesn't Understand, Megan Devine (Sound True, Inc., 2017). This book debunks the culturally prescribed goal of returning to a normal, "happy" life, replacing it with a far healthier middle path, one that invites us to build a life alongside grief rather than seeking to overcome it.

Shattered: Surviving the Loss of a Child, Gary Roe (CreateSpace Independent Publishing Platform, 2017). This is a heartfelt, easy-to-read, and intensely practical book which walks the reader through the powerful impact a child's death can have—emotionally, mentally, physically, relationally, and spiritually.

ABOUT THE AUTHORS

Ed Lee is co-founder and partner of Wahoo's Fish Taco, responsible for the expansion and development of what has become one of the most iconic fast-casual restaurant brands in the United States. With more than 40 years of experience in the restaurant and hospitality industry, he has helped his co-founding brothers Wing Lam and Mingo Lee establish Wahoo's as a pop culture mainstay in California and beyond.

He also co-founded Our House Coffee Shop and Night Club, Schroff Clothing, Kitsch Bar, Rooster Cafe, Tackle Box, Toast Kitchen & Bakery, Fill Bakeshop, and Tableau Kitchen & Bar. He started a company called Seven Hour Drive that makes a patented water-saving device for restaurants and commercial kitchens

Ed is frequently invited to speak and give lectures at various universities including University of Southern California, University of California, Irvine, and his alma mater Vanguard University, where he earned a Bachelor of Arts in Business. He is on the Board of Vocational Visions, which helps disabled adults get jobs, and the Board of UCI's Antrepreneur, which provides resources for students interested in innovation and entrepreneurship.

In 2018, Ed was named One of OC's Most Influential by the *Orange County Register* and was written up in the same publication a year later as being "The Restaurant Whisperer" for his extensive mentoring of young restaurateurs. He was nominated as Entrepreneur of the Year by the *Orange County Business Journal*, and in 2022, he was named Restaurateur of the Year by the *Journal*.

He has been married to his wife, Michal, since 1994 and together they raised two sons.

Ronald K. Ottenad is the founder of Rooted Soul Ministries, which seeks to create environments where people encounter God and learn to walk in freedom. He also serves as a Staff Spiritual Director at the Center for Spiritual Renewal, in La Mirada, CA, and Adjunct Professor at Talbot School of Theology. He served as a pastor in a large church in Southern California for 21 years. He has a Bachelor of Arts Degree in Journalism from California State University Long Beach, and two Master of Arts Degrees from Biola University, Organizational Leadership and Spiritual Formation and Soul Care. He has written three other books: *The Good Way: Walking an Old Road to a New Life*, *The Ascent to Santiago: A Contemplative Journal for Those Walking the Way of Saint James* and *The Risk Men: The Unexpected Rewards of Lifelong Friendship*. He has been happily married to his wife, Tammie, since 1987 and has two adult children.

Made in the USA
Middletown, DE
28 October 2022

13696874R00088